the beast in the temple

James Gibb Stuart

William Maclellan (Embryo) Ltd.

First Published 1982

ISBN 0 85335 2534 (Cased)
ISBN 0 85335 2542 (Paperback)

Published by William Maclellan (Embryo) Ltd.
268 Bath Street, Glasgow, G2 4JR

Produced by
Eric Moore & Company
27 Brown Street, Glasgow G2 8PE

CONTENTS

FOREWORD

It seems to the author that for the best part of a lifetime Christians and the Christian faith have been on the defensive. Confronted by a challenge from the secular philosophies which have dominated social and religious thinking throughout the second half of the twentieth century, the Church has felt increasingly ill at ease with its role in a technological society, and has continuously given ground.

Does it matter? That is a question which is asked in a variety of ways, and in a diversity of situations, in the chapters that follow.

Does it matter? to the parson or the priest? to their flocks in kirk or parish or chapel? to the swelling majority of ordinary folk who have lost all contact with religion, and come to regard it as an irrelevance in their workaday lives?

The question should not be dismissed too lightly, nor the answer spiced with a derisory two-finger salute. For this is no exercise in abstract religious theory, to be debated and argued over by cloistered monks or theological seminaries. To paraphrase a title from the bibliography, it is in fact *all about you,* about the problems of modern-day living, protection of hearth and home, providing a stable future for our children, — with a positive bearing upon whether our children have a future at all.

As was hinted in "The Mind Benders", there is a great deal of guff and gobbledegook in our popular misconceptions of the essential issues. Under the still expanding influence of press and television, it has become frighteningly easy for the opinion moulders to put their own superficial slant on politics, economics and even religion, — and those who search beneath the surface, who sense the fallacies that lurk beyond the trivia, are often confounded by a public apathy which rejects uncomfortable fact in favour of socially acceptable legend.

Once again, does it matter? And are you quite clear on the implications if we continue to stand aside and let the evolutionary philosophies inherit the Kingdom? If not, there could be a message for you here, since *that* is what *The Beast in the Temple* is all about.

"Blessed are ye when men shall revile you, and persecute you, and shall say all manner of evil against you falsely, for my sake."
St. Matthew 5:11

CHAPTER I

¶ 1 THE PARAMETERS OF PRAYER

What's to prayer these days? that is, if we believe in prayer at all. The long formal perorations uttered in church services by the local parson! or the hasty semi-coherent offerings thrown up in desperation to an Unseen Presence at times of mortal danger and anxiety? Apart from the clergy, for whom public prayer is a part of their calling, how many people pray nowadays, as an integral part of their faith and their spiritual lives? Also, what are the parameters within which it is recognised as legitimate to invoke the Almighty? The threatened death of a child perhaps? Or in an attempt to ward off disaster from one's home or family? Not the prospect of pecuniary gain! And certainly not for the purpose of stealing an advantage! The Lord does not take sides, or assist in grudge fights. There are rules which one learns as one goes along.

But within these rules, does prayer work? Can it be seen to work? Or is its efficacy more apparent to the devout suppliant than to the uncommitted bystander?

¶ 2 A TIME AND PLACE FOR EVERYTHING

A long-dead Church of Scotland minister used to love telling the tale of a God-fearing ship's captain who held services on deck every Sunday morning, and hinted to his passengers that he would pray for them if they attended, but could not guarantee to remember them in their absence. Some came, others stayed away, and it was not unusual for the old mariner to go through his devotions against a background of light-hearted laughter as the more active members of the ship's complement took advantage of the morning sunshine for a round of shipboard sports.

Once when the devout old seafarer was taking his charge home through the Bay of Biscay, he ran into an unexpected squall. The sky darkened, the wind rose, the sea came at him in mountainous waves which broke over the bows and cascaded across the decks. The boat strained and creaked at every plate and timber, and as the storm went on for hour after hour with little sign of abatement, many of the less experienced passengers began to fear for their safety. Some braved the conditions to join the captain on his bridge, where they appealed to him to pray for them. He was a stern Presbyterian, a West Highlandman no doubt, and as he looked at their anxious faces he saw amongst them a number who had scorned his invitation to Sunday morning worship. So he told them that there was a time for prayer, as there was a time for everything else. *His* time had been when the sea was calm, and shipboard matters were under control. But when the wind rose, and the waves were beating at him, he needed all his concentration for the steering of the ship.

¶ 3 "MAN THAT DIED FOR MEN"

All right! so you have a limited tolerance for bible-punching West Highland sea captains who tend to ram their Calvanistic principles down the throats of the unrighteous. You decide that however you might have spent your time in that particular ship's company, you would have tried to stay away at all costs from the morning sermons on the boat deck. In which case how would *you* have reacted to the imminent prospect of shipwreck and a watery grave? When in fact would *you* start praying,—that is, if you believe in prayer at all?

Funny thing, isn't it? Down through the centuries every generation has had its share of agnostics, heretics and blasphemers,—perversely non-conforming individuals who delighted in slamming both the spiritual and the temporal powers, and in less tolerant ages would often do so at considerable risk to their personal freedoms. But their profanities, either punishable or tolerated, were generally regarded as a pose and a demonstration, something in which the professing heretic would indulge for the confusion and the scandalising of his self-righteous associates. It had nothing to do with the eventual relationship between himself and his Maker. Face to face with eternity, many an apparent non-believer passed over into the hereafter with a prayer on his lips and repentance in his heart.

It helped if the occasion involved some element of self-sacrifice,—as with the irreverent little wartime deckhand who was reckoned to have saved his ship when he deflected a magnetic mine and blew himself up in the process.

"He saw his duty a dead sure thing,
And he went for it there an' then;
An' sure Christ ain't gonna be too hard
On a man that died for men."

¶ 4 THE CHRISTIAN AS AN ADVENTURER

A remarkable feature about the God-fearing is that in many cases they fear little else. The great feats of adventure and exploration in the last century,—the penetration of savage jungles, scaling of ice-bound peaks and taming of desert wastes,—were the dedicated pursuit of men who knew their bibles as they knew the palms of their hands. David Livingstone and Captain Cook, the pioneers of America's covered waggons and the voortrekkers of South Africa in their epic journey across the Vaal,—all possessed that courage and resolution in face of the unknown which springs from a deep and abiding faith, a trust in the righteousness and consistency of an Almighty Being whom they felt to be watching over them even in the midst of stormy seas or the infinity of trackless deserts.

The carpers and the hypocrites, the Satanists and the inveterate non-believers, always seemed to get left behind in the planning of such unpredictable and dangerous enterprises. Much more appealing to them the habitats of civilised man, the settled places and the social pursuits in which one was less likely to have his courage tested!

Not to say, of course, that the men who blazed the trails, hacked their way through the jungles and sailed the distant oceans went forward to a chorus of hallelujahs, and quotations from the shorter catechism! Most likely their language was profane, and in moments of stress or boredom they consoled themselves with many a ribald jest, cursing both the God above and the Devil beneath for their pains and their privations. But in the extremity they were still believers, praying in the night and in lonely places because they dared not share their innermost thoughts with their fellows. And when they faced death,—as they often did,—either from famine or tempest, or at the end of a loaded gun, it was as Christians that they stood up to the ultimate challenge, reconciled to their fate on earth, and the promise of a life hereafter. If they had time for it, and if they could find the words, invariably they prayed.

¶ 5 THE DOCTRINE OF UNBELIEF

But even at this early stage you might be saying to yourself, what's this guy's fixation with prayer, and his concern with the twelfth-hour affirmations of hard-bitten adventurers in remote and dangerous corners of the globe? After all, he's probably not that much built up on prayer himself,—and he doesn't sound like the stock version of a creeping Jesus. So where does he hope to get with all this religious stuff in a secular age where the prevailing wisdom is to deliver a horse-laugh against any suggestion of divine guidance?

Well that's it, as a matter of fact. Those hedonist agnostics who set the modern fashion are totally unlike the profaners and blasphemers of an earlier age, whose heresies found no favour in society at large, and who were normally content to be left alone in irreverent obscurity.

The present day atheist and agnostic on the other hand have a passionate commitment to their unbelief, have even upgraded it to the conception of a pragmatic Earthbound religion. Neither are they confined to the ranks of the under-privileged, the misfits or the woefully misinformed. The new generation of anti-God cultists is a race of academic, scientifically-orientated sophisticates who reckon that reason, mathematics and computer science have comfortably superseded the Sermon on the Mount and the gospels of Matthew, Mark, Luke and John. Such people are no longer confined to the fringes of society. They have come to occupy its centre, and what they say, what they feel and decide, are now in many cases the established norm. It is something about which we should have received clear and adequate notice before it happened or whilst it was happening, but in fact it has taken place so quietly and surreptitiously that relatively few are aware that it has happened at all.

It's a kind of covert revolution,—not a constitutional revolution involving the expropriation of established powers,—but a revolution in thought, a philosophical turnabout whose motives and ultimate objectives have been concealed from all but the initiates. And of course it had to be of more recent date than that old Presbyterian story about the cruise ship and its devout captain, who knew how to pray, but who kept his hands on the wheel and his mind on the storm as the waves were breaking over his bows. In that ship's company there were some who, in calm seas and sunshine, had shunned the old man's divine service because there were so many more interesting and more pleasant things for them to do. Yet when disaster threatened, and they began to fear for their lives, instinctively they put aside their shame and their embarrassment and asked the captain to pray for them.

What then of this new breed of scientific and technological materialists? Since their central belief is one of non-belief, they would surely have deemed it a basic heresy, even in the gravest peril, to appeal to any supernatural Being for salvation and reassurance. So *they* could not have asked the captain to pray for them,—not when the whole essence of their philosophy was that there was no one to whom prayer could be offered. So what would they do, how would they react, those reasoning and rationalising elitists,—scared as they might be like anyone else in the midst of the holocaust? To whom or to what would they turn in the face of extreme and terrifying danger?

¶ 6 EARTH'S MOST IMPORTANT SPECIES

It's an intriguing question, folks. Anyone quick to come up with the answer? Anyone amongst us know instinctively, or from experience, how the non-theist deals with those moments of distress and extreme pressure in which a Christian would resort to prayer? You will see, as you progress through the pages of this book, that we have posed ourselves a cruncher right at the beginning. We have touched upon a matter which could have a vital bearing on our future, and that of our children.

Why? Because this new breed of scientific materialists, these heretical prophets of non-belief, are bidding fair to make themselves the most important species upon the face of the Earth. They control the policies of governments and multinational corporations, the faculties of famous universities, the editorial boards of syndicated newspapers and the broadcasting facilities of radio and television networks.

They call themselves *humanists,* after the manner of those who thought to serve humanity by a study of Greek and Roman culture. That is not to say that modern humanism has much to do with humanitarianism,—though its practitioners proclaim their tolerance and concern for mankind as a considerable virtue. As for the breathtaking assertion that any coordinated group of men and women,—any single philosophy,—might wield such fantastic power and influence,—well, hear us out. Suspend judgment until you have read a bit of the story, which begins with the publication of the First Humanist Manifesto in 1933.

CHAPTER II

¶ 7 THE FIRST HUMANIST MANIFESTO

So what kind of an epoch-shattering event was that? Not much, in terms of the contemporary world, which largely ignored it! Appearing in the early summer of 1933, in the pages of a little-known periodical called *The New Humanist,*—which was presumably lying handy for just such a purpose,—this initial affirmation of humanist intent and principles was subscribed by a number of socio-political and politico-academic individuals in British-American society such as John Dewey, Robert Morss Levett, R. Lester Mondale and David Rhys Williams.

A document of some fifteen clauses, that first manifesto,—so little publicised, and yet fraught with such ultimate significance,—tended to polarise the range of secular feelings that had been germinated in the wake of Darwinism, and came down in favour of an *evolutionary* basis for man's origins rather than his conception through the impetus of a Supreme Being.

In Clause Two, for instance, those early humanists insisted that "man is a part of nature", and "has emerged as the result of a continuous process". Their subsequent thought is that "the traditional dualism of mind and body",—i.e. earthly body and immortal soul,—"must be rejected", and by the Seventh Clause they are laying the basis of a new religion which would embrace everything which is "humanly significant", including labour, art, science, philosophy, love, friendship and recreation. The distinction between the sacred and the secular, they said, could no longer be maintained.

Clause Nine: In place of the old attitudes involved in worship and prayer, the humanist finds his religious emotions expressed in a heightened sense of personal life and in a cooperative effort to promote social well-being.

Clause Ten: It follows that there will be no uniquely religious emotions and attitudes of the kind hitherto associated with belief in the supernatural.

Clause Twelve: Believing that religion must work increasingly for joy in living, religious humanists aim to foster the creative in man, and to encourage achievements that add to the satisfactions of life.

¶ 8 ANOTHER MEIN KAMPF

Well, who could argue with that? The subscribers to the Manifesto were taking a sly sideswipe at the established religions of their day, and hinting that they had not done all they could towards the cultivation of human happiness. But notice another thing! Those advocates of a twentieth century apostasy did not at that early stage emphasise their affinity with atheism, agnosticism and all the kindred creeds based on a denial of divine initiative. What they tried to insinuate was that their rejection of the fundamentals of the Christian faith did not imply any rebuttal of religious values. Drawing upon their fund of technological expertise, plus a bit of common-or-garden legerdemain and applied psychology, they were proposing to go on enjoying all the unique features and refinements of the superstructure whilst keeping it in a state of indefinite suspension,—following upon an entire removal of the foundation layers, and even a blasting of the primeval rock upon which the Church was reputedly constructed.

The observance devoid of original meaning! The form without the substance! Whilst dispensing with the divine impulses and inspirations of the Christian religion, those early humanists did not intend to dispense with religion itself. Theirs was to be a *religious* form of humanism that would maintain *all associations and institutions* that *exist for the fulfilment of human life,*—including of course the ecclesiastical structures passed down to us by our Christian forefathers. But "religious institutions, their ritualistic forms, ecclesiastical methods and communal activities must be reconstituted as rapidly as experience allows, in order to function effectively in the modern world". (First Humanist Manifesto, Clause Thirteen.)

Get the drift of that one, please! Read it slowly. And if the meaning doesn't dawn on you the first time, read it again till you grasp its full import. Having told us, as they did in their preamble to the 1933 Manifesto, that Christian "doctrines and methods . . . have lost their significance and . . . are powerless to solve the problems of human living in the Twentieth Century", the humanists will not necessarily be content to let us amble along in our old traditional ways, till our faith and our beliefs atrophy under their own irrelevance. They give very clear warning that they intend to muscle in on our "religious institutions and ritualistic forms", reconstituting them "as rapidly as experience allows", so that they will conform to the humanistic world of the future.

In view of what we shall subsequently have to reveal about humanist influences upon Western churches, this might almost be taken as a prophetic declaration, a sort of humanist "Mein Kampf". And it will be found, as in "Mein Kampf", that a considerable part of the prospectus has already been fulfilled ere we are aware of what is happening.

¶ 9 THE NON-PROFIT-MAKING SOCIETY

Something else they said away back there in 1933. Clause Fourteen stated that "existing acquisitive and profit-making society had shown itself to be inadequate and that a radical change in methods, controls and motives must be instituted. A social and cooperative economic order must be established to the end that the equitable distribution of the means of life be possible. The goal of humanism is a free and universal society in which people voluntarily and intelligently cooperate for the common good."

Nothing new and dramatically refreshing about that one, is there? It's what the socialists have been trying to achieve since they were first given a chance to hold the reins of government. And the more socialism they introduce, the more the economic situation deteriorates. As for that stuff about "acquisitive and profit-making society", it has been clearly illustrated in the traumatic conditions of the late twentieth century that a sure formula for collapsing living standards and evaporation of the wealth of nations is the establishment of non-profit-making service and manufacturing industries allegedly cooperating for the common good.

Even so, whilst committing the heresy of denying the Creator, that early Humanist Manifesto had scarcely set down a recipe for mayhem and universal terror. Or had it? Fairly modest and overbearingly reasonable in all its precepts and avowed intentions! Humanists insisted on change, but they also affirmed their adherence to democracy, and abjured violence. Change must come peacefully.

After those earlier centuries of intolerance and religious persecution, it might even have seemed calming and reassuring that this new superior breed intended to go about their work pacifically, and without unwonted persuasion. There were times,—not so far distant,— when religious change had literally been washed in innocent blood.

So for those Christians who were immediately aware of the humanists' proposals, perhaps there were no flashing early warning signals, no clarion calls to arms and to a spirited defence of the faith. For what was it to be defended against? Just the mild-mannered assertions and postulations of a bunch of academic sophisticates, college professors, professional educators, social philosophers and obscure politicians who thought they could change society by a process of scientific reasoning, and a paramount belief in man's ability to achieve his greatest goals unaided by inspiration from above.

Yet the purpose of this book, with its challenging and forbidding title, is to demonstrate how the birth of this reasoning and apparently tolerant philosophy may conceivably have been responsible for much of the social unrest, terror and violence that has marred the latter part of the twentieth century.

¶ 10 VIOLENCE AND MIND CONTROL

We are once again living in a violent age. It did not need to be so. With improvements in communications, and with rising living standards across vast areas of the globe, there seemed so much scope for greater understanding, enhanced opportunities for nations, and factions within those nations, to talk out their rivalries and their differences, rather than have them settled by the gun or the bomb. But along the way something went wrong,and in too many parts of the world an outmoded savagery has taken the place of earlier civilising influences. What particular belief,—or cult,— or dynasty has thrust back our promised age of enlightenment, so that even in sophisticated Western cities there are areas where the weak and elderly live in fear,—and where unescorted women dare not venture abroad at night?

Well, it's easy to reach back into both near and more distant memory and bring forth examples of cults and ideologies which have prospered by fear and intimidation, and the total extinction of individual liberties. The infamous Stalinist purges in Russia of the 1930's! The gruesome atrocities practised in the death camps of Nazi Germany during the Second World War! Exploitation! Starvation! The use of human bodies as guinea pigs for way-out experiments in human mutation! The clinical use of mind drugs,—thought drugs! The beginnings of that nightmarish advance in medical technology,—much more sophisticated than anything the Spanish Inquisition had to offer,—whereby a human being could have his beliefs, his traditions and his innate desires and affiliations destroyed, only to have them supplanted by an alien belief and code of morality!

¶ 11 PUNISHING THE NAZIS

From time to time this volume may have cause to comment upon the strange silences and aberrations of the mass communications industry anent events and manifestations which have portentous significance for the future of our society. But no one could have complained about the thoroughness with which the Western press set about the total annihilation of Nazi *herrenvolk* principles and ideals once the extent of their brutalities in Occupied Europe became better known. A sensation of relief and thankfulness was bruited abroad after the final collapse of the totalitarian empire which at one stage had threatened to dominate our continent for generations. And at the Nuremberg Trials a year or two later, there was a self-righteous clamour for stern justice and revenge upon the captured hierarchs of a creed which had allegedly taught the world new standards in barbarism. It was as though all good and evil had been brought into stark juxtaposition at those tribunals, with the good inalienably established upon the side of the prosecutors, the judges and the victims, — the evil hovering like a noxious cloud around the prisoners in the dock who stood arraigned on charges of plunder, torture, sustained brutalities and mass genocide. The citizens of allied countries who had so recently known the privations and indignities of military occupation, as well as those nations who had escaped a similar fate either by geographical circumstance or their own considerable exertions, rejoiced in their hearts that *right* had been so thoroughly vindicated, whilst *wrong* was about to be subjected to the condign punishments which it so properly deserved.

It was possible to believe, in the spirit of the times, that with the defeat of Nazism, humanity stood on the threshold of a new age of tolerance and enlightenment. We had seen the mark of the Beast, and had rejoiced in his annihilation. We had survived the rigours and the uncertainties of our Armageddon. Now God was back in his Heaven,— and all was coming right with the world.

¶ 12 SLAVES OF STALIN'S RUSSIA

Was that it? Was that truly the spirit of those early post-war years? Had we been so obsessed with the evils and injustices of the Nazi system, and our struggles to contain and overcome them, that nothing else seemed to be of a comparable significance? With the institution of a world body dedicated to the ideal of peace and justice for all men of all creeds and all colours, did we in fact allow ourselves, even for a short period, to believe that civilisation had embarked upon a new golden age?

If so, it must have been easier to accept it in the better class suburbs of Birmingham and Baltimore than in cities like Bialystok and Budapest, where expurgation of the Nazi tyranny had not resulted in an early restoration of civic and individual freedoms. And to those many thousands of displaced persons who survived Hitler's Third Reich only to be forcibly deported back across the frontiers into Stalin's Russia, it must have been immediately apparent that they had escaped from one totalitarian regime just to be swallowed up by another.

There would be no point in endeavouring to catalogue here the heartrending stories of torture, deprivation and execution which took place in Eastern Europe following the inexplicable release of so many of Hitler's war victims into the Soviets' ungentle hands. That episode will for ever be a blot upon the names of the Western statesmen who knew about it, yet still allowed it to happen. Suffice it that the peace settlement put together at Potsdam between Roosevelt and Stalin not only allowed the latter a free hand in the disciplining of those elements who had thought to make a permanent escape from his prison house, — it also gave him legitimacy and opportunity for a vast export of terror and intimidation beyond his own borders.

Even in Birmingham and Baltimore, — as in Bournemouth and Bridlington, Boston and Bardstown, Kentucky, — the message would get through eventually. Tyranny, torture and persecution had not vanished from the earth with the eclipse and downfall of the Third Reich. They had gone under cover for a time, only to emerge more virulent, more vindictive than before. Westerners could look on from a distance and be truly thankful for their own congenial environment, but for several millions of long-suffering unfortunate souls trapped within the ramifications of the Soviet slave camp and penal system, those years after the Second World War must have seemed like a continuing nightmare that might endure for ever.

¶ 13 WHAT NAZIS AND COMMUNISTS HAD IN COMMON

So when we reckon how the twentieth century has failed to live up to its early promise of an age blessed in tolerance and understanding, we have to take account of the two militant philosophies whose excesses and overreaching ambitions have contributed so much to the toll in human misery that has been exacted both between and after the great wars. And when we examine those two ideologies, — which to the immature and simple-minded may seem to have an unbridgeable gulf between them, — we find that they had one thing in common. Yes, the Nazis of Hitler's Germany and the Communists of Soviet Russia had one essential and fundamental thing in common, — a rebuttal of, and a departure from, the doctrines of Jesus Christ.

Presupposing therefore that the tortures, brainwashings and

Stuffing Christ into the garbage bin, — what Nazis, Communists and humanists have in common.

massacres had been foreseen by long-sighted Nazi and Communist ideologists as necessary for the imposition and maintenance of their totalitarian systems, — it may now become apparent that this renunciation of Christian standards and values was in fact the first and unavoidable step towards the tyrannies which they had in mind. Before wiping out all forms of social and political opposition, they had initially to brutalise the morals and sensibilities of those who would implement their plans. After all, Hitler could scarcely have expected to staff his Jewish death camps with lay preachers and hymn-singing devotees of the Lutheran Protestant Church, all of whose Christian upbringing and moral principles would have been outraged by such a monstrous assault on human dignity.

Likewise the Machiavellian activities of the Russian KGB, the dedication to a long-term campaign of subversion, treachery, double-dealing, corruption of men's minds, morals, motives and innermost yearnings, — the imposition and administration of slave labour camps, psychiatric prisons and penal colonies that plumb the depths of human degradation, — could not be implemented with the ready compliance of Christian men and women who carried in their hearts any concept of divine justice, and who owed loyalty to anything over and above the System in which they had become enmeshed.

As to that new species of scientific and medical practitioner who specialises in the technique of mind-control through drugs, whose particular function is to work upon the thought processes of awkward and non-conforming elements within society, — who occasionally turns a brilliant well-balanced thinking human being into a mindless vegetable, and whose application of know-how and experience to such despicable aims and practices is a total travesty of the healing art of medicine, — he is unlikely to pursue such heinous experiments in tandem with an eldership at the local Orthodox Church. Or if he does, how can he reconcile his professional calling with his religious principles when the Ministry of Justice sends in one of his own preachers for anti-deviationist therapy to eradicate dangerous delusions about the existence of a Supreme Being?

Interesting thought, isn't it? Maybe you hadn't thought of it that way before. But you really ought to think on it now,—that the totalitarian excesses, the brutalities, executions and mind-numbing atrocities of Nazism and Marxist-Communism which have marred the last half-century of mankind's stumbling and uncertain progress, were only made possible in their all-embracing horror because Christ's message and teachings, His emphasis on mercy and human dignity, His call to salvation and redemption in the after-life, had first of all been eradicated from men's minds, and substituted by a racialist or hate-filled class ideology that had within it all the nastinesses and the weaknesses of mortal man.

¶ 14 REMOVING THE CHRISTIAN FACTOR

The humanists also limit their vision and expectations to what can be achieved by mortal man, — though apparently not for purposes of totalitarian repression. In fact the first and foremost goal of the humanistic philosophy is expressed as an expansion and an enlargement of man's outlook and potentialities, rather than his mental imprisonment and confinement within some ideological mould. Tolerance is the stated watchword of all their policy-making and problem-rationalising. They are desirous of change, but eloquent upon the need for that change to come gradually and peacefully, in a manner acceptable to the vast majority of mankind. Not for them, they say, the torture cells and the slave camps, the mind drugs and the insanity clinics; the violent treatment of dissident elements and the elimination of inconvenient and non-conforming minorities!

They even lay claims to achieve change and human progress without the bigotries and inter-denominational rivalries which have sullied the reputation of the Holy Christian Church. The Humanist Revolution would be a peaceful revolution, a triumph of universal consent, a gradualist conversion and adjustment of men's minds to a new philosophy and a new way of living. That was what they maintained in both their manifestos.

So, 'twixt the Nazi cult of race supremacy, the Communist straitjacket of total conformity, and the humanistic emphasis on reason and scientific values, there was allegedly a world of difference. Only in one significant respect did they seem to come together. They had but one thing in common, — that in their fundamental appraisal of man's place on earth, they scorned all notions of divine inspiration, or worship or obedience to an Almighty God.

¶ 15 THE FUNDAMENTAL DIFFERENCE

Having come to their various conclusions that religion was just so much irrelevant mumbo-jumbo, an outmoded relic from a primitive past, they went about their denials and their renunciations in different ways. The Nazis gleaned from the Christian doctrine all that could be adapted to their own style of thinking, and discarded everything which was unfavourable or contradictory. During the Bolshevik Revolution the Marxists had consolidated their conquest by executing the priests and burning down the churches, and though their later methods were more circumspect, they continued to harry and brutally persecute fundamentalist sects and dissident individuals who would not compromise their beliefs.

The humanists on the other hand, having their main power base within the Western democracies, were never in a position to institute draconian measures against those who disagreed with them, but they insisted that such was not their purpose in any case. They had, they said, positively no intention of wiping out or suppressing established religions. In fact they had from the beginning gone out of their way to seek cooperation and association with practising Christians in many areas where their aims might be seen to coincide. They formed societies of religious humanists, invited liberal-minded churchmen to join them, established churches of their own, and generally connived at such an integration and an overlapping of customs and observances that it became difficult to distinguish one from the other. Humanists in the main were such nice reasonable and respectable people that even the most closely knit Christian community might find it hard to justify continuing suspicion and antagonism.

Even so, for all the socialising and the coincidence of aims and purposes, there remained that one fundamental issue, — that Christians believe in the divinity and teachings of Jesus Christ, in His mission on earth and His promise of a life hereafter. The humanists do *not* so believe. They claim that the advance of science and technology, the conquest of space and man's ever-increasing control over his environment, have made God redundant, — and that aspirations towards an ultimate salvation are a harmful diversion, filling people's minds with false hopes of an illusory Heaven.

¶ 16 CHRISTENDOM'S AWESOME RESPONSIBILITY

So here we have this cruncher at such an early stage in the proceedings. We have to make a decision, — and we have to get it right, — not only for ourselves, but for mankind as a whole.

Why? Because due to the dynamic inspiration of Christian teaching and disciplines down through the ages, Christendom has become the main repository of advanced human knowledge and the principal vehicle of man's social, political and technological progress. We may appreciate it or we may not, — but we are the torchbearers for that culture and civilisation which was handed down by Greece and Rome, and which almost alone has fought the battle against primitive savagery, superstition and ignorance. Albeit the flame has flickered uncertainly in recent years. Due to our own inward doubts and questionings, we have at times given a confused and fumbling lead, have occasionally brought despair to millions for whom we must be the only hope of an emancipated future. So if we fail, if we take a wrong turning, if the torch should fall into other hands or its light be finally extinguished, then it may be that we shall have set the world on a stumbling retreat back towards the Dark Ages.

Now to the cruncher! What we have to decide is whether Christianity plus humanism is a full and adequate answer to the menace of Marxist-Soviet totalitarianism, — whether in fact we should embrace those nice humanist guys for their tolerance and their eminent respectability, — or sticking to fundamentals, should shun them as non-believers who could never at any time be relied upon to assist in the defence of our faith.

And whilst we are all pondering our own particular solutions to that conundrum, let us not forget that this atheism, this agnosticism, this profaning and negation of the divine beliefs is what the humanists, the Nazis and the Communists have all had in common. Have we nevertheless to judge the humanists differently because they seem tolerant in their scepticism, and because it is hard to imagine them making common cause with Nazi or Communist totalitarianism?

All right! you need time to think that one over. You also need to know much more about the humanists and their plans for a new world order. Settle yourself in a comfortable chair. The knowledge will be duly forthcoming. We are about to do a rundown on a bunch of shy retiring characters who seldom advertise what they are thinking and doing, yet whose influence on our own and future generations might be totally out of proportion to their numbers.

CHAPTER III

¶ 17 THE EVOLUTIONARY THEORY

How about Charles Darwin and "The Origin of Species"? Swallowed it all entirely? Or are you just a bit bothered that after all those years no one amongst his many disciples has ever been able to track down the missing link?

The concept of evolution from single cell creatures up to the infinite complexities of modern man, — that plus the highly romanticised search for confirmatory evidence in the higher echelons of the animal kingdom, — has absorbed the attention of more than one generation of philosophers, geneticists and anthropologists, and laid the groundwork for that questioning of traditional values which mathematics and astronomy had already put in jeopardy through their unravelling of so many of the secrets of the universe. To many a scientific mind, trained in the art of step-by-step deduction, and disinclined to accept anything which could not be explained by reason and calculation, the ritualistic belief in a hymn-singing Heaven hidden somewhere up there behind a bank of stratocumulus, was something that should have gone out with the candle and the wooden plough.

As for the conquest of space, where was God going to hide when intrepid man had set his feet upon the planets?

¶ 18 AN EARLY HUMANIST ELITE

The humanists were to build upon both the evolutionary theory and scientific methods of deduction. Even so they did not openly deride or debunk orthodox religious sentiments, merely criticising them as too rigid or too restrictive for the modern stage of man's development. To quote Clause Fifteen of the 1933 Manifesto, they considered the religious forms and ideas of our fathers to be no longer adequate. Man was "at last becoming aware that he alone was responsible for the realisation of the world of his dreams, that he had within himself the power for its achievement."

The new creed attracted many of the clever people, the intelligentsia, the professors and the college dons, the chemists and the physicists who were fascinated by the manner in which they and their recent predecessors had advanced the frontiers of human knowledge.

Unlike the atheism, the heresies and the agnosticism of previous centuries, humanism achieved an early respectability, finding converts throughout the elite of society and in some of the highest posts in the land. Prominent amongst its first supporters were Professor Julian Huxley, the Scottish lords Boyd Orr and Ritchie Calder, and the English philosopher Bertrand Russell. George Bernard Shaw, the Webbs and many other members of the British Fabian Society were soul mates and travelling companions from the beginning. On the other side of the Atlantic, American Fabians John Dewey and Robert Morss Lovett were, as noted, original signatories to the 1933 Manifesto, and Eleanor Roosevelt, wife of America's wartime president, — herself a convert to the new philosophy, — saw to it that its secular urbanities were well represented in the White House.

The sardonic French philosopher Jean-Paul Sartre was a humanist, so also was the well-known commentator and broadcaster Malcolm Muggeridge, — until a late conversion to Roman Catholicism set him on a frantic race to restore much of the faith and tradition which his humanist *alter ego* had debunked and partially destroyed.

¶ 19 MOVING INTO POSITIONS OF POWER

Now at this point you might just be excused for thinking that the exercise upon which we are embarked is somewhat academic, — like studying the North Country boll weevil or the nocturnal peregrinations of the Cotswold feathered owl. After all, you might be saying to yourself, those early humanists weren't actually *bothering* anyone, were they? A scholarly, deep-thinking bunch for the most part! Quiet, respectable, law-abiding! Scarcely the sort to start a punch-up at the local, or rip the seats of passenger trains in the aftermath of a football match!

So why make such a fuss about their doings and their deliberations if they weren't interfering with us? True that their materialistic ideas were spreading throughout the professional and academic worlds like marking ink sopping into a sponge! But they weren't trying to *force* themselves on us, were they? You and I, who had gone our way believing after a fashion in the eternal values of Heaven and the hereafter, were not being constrained or pressurised into dropping our faith, our customs or our adherences. We were encouraged to assume that there could be a kind of co-existence as between the spiritual and the secular, the religious and the profane.

And as it happened, we were not to receive much warning of the influence which humanistic beliefs and doctrines would have upon the history of the second half of the twentieth century. Those early humanists, like their colleagues and close collaborators the Fabians, were birds of rare plumage who hesitated to disport themselves in public. And as with the Fabians, their capacity for mass persuasion and manipulation would usher them into positions of awe-inspiring power.

¶ 20 THE RELIGION OF THE 21st CENTURY

The Second Humanist Manifesto was published in the autumn of 1973, and was a much more detailed, more comprehensive and more confident document than its predecessor of forty years earlier. Its promoters expanded on the viewpoint that modern technological man had outgrown the concept of an all-seeing, prayer-hearing God, and should be looking to other means for his salvation and survival. They argued that humanity needed to extend the uses of scientific method, and to fuse reason with compassion in order to build constructive social and moral values. The ultimate goal was to be the fulfilment of potential in each human personality, — not for the favoured few, — but for all mankind.

They identified many kinds of humanism as currently existing in the contemporary world. Amongst such were the scientific, the ethical, the democratic, the religious and the *Marxist* types of humanism. Atheism, agnosticism, scepticism, deism and liberal religion were all claimed to be rooted in the humanistic tradition, — though it was emphasised that a *mere renunciation of divine belief* did not in itself constitute a commitment to humanism, which had to be based upon a positive conviction of human progress within the framework of humanistic values.

Grandly too, those architects of the Second Manifesto proclaimed that the twenty-first century belonged to them. Using technology wisely, the new generation of humanists would control the environment, conquer disease, extend the lifespan, provide us all with "unparalleled opportunity for achieving an abundant and a meaningful life". Through a marshalling of all the massive agricultural, medical and economic technology available within the Western developed nations, they planned an eventual assault upon the causes of world poverty, — and they intended that disproportions of wealth, income and economic growth should be levelled out, both between nations and between social classes within those nations.

¶ 21 ANY FAITH, OR NO FAITH AT ALL

What could be nobler and more altruistic than that? How many people, — handed such a document and given time to study it, — could have objected to putting their signatures upon such a glowing and idealistic vision for the future? Hundreds of good-living, well-educated and eminently placed citizens of both Britain and America did indeed sign it, — either then or subsequently, — as they embraced its unexceptionable ideals. Amongst them were some seventy-five professors and lecturers of worldwide universities, a smattering of medical doctors and a hundred and seventy ministers of the Universalist and Unitarian Churches. These latter, by the way, were not denying their vows, since it is apparently a tenet of both the Unitarians and the Universalists that they will accept *any* belief and *no* belief on the part of their members.

For those who are curious about such a laxity of doctrinal commitment in the ritual of two established churches, Claire Chambers notes in "The SIECUS Circle" that approximately a quarter of the signatories to the First Humanist Manifesto were also Unitarians, — *which helps us to an understanding of what was going on during those forty years, and for that matter has been going on ever since.*

Chambers quotes Edwin H. Wilson, a former director of the American Humanist Association, as claiming that the AHA "stemmed largely from Unitarianism as a movement of religious humanists." So the humanists, having outlived the usefulness of a divine belief and a prayer-hearing God, still wanted to have all the customs, the ceremony and the observances of church worship, even though for them there could be no confession of faith, no commitment to a higher life, no promise of salvation in a life hereafter.

The author has no idea how the Unitarian-Universalists conduct their services, — what hymns they sing, what prayers they offer, and to whom or what they dedicate their devotions. But he can see very clearly, — as hopefully can most of his readers, — what purpose can be served by having a number of mock religious bodies closely affiliated to humanism. Their aim was to present this godless materialistic creed as a religion, — the religion which in course of time would swallow all other religions, which would in fact become the ecclesiastical symbol of the future.

¶ 22 FORWARD THE ECUMENICALS

So we've reached another stage, haven't we? We're trying to take this deliberately, step by step, so that nothing gets missed as we go along.

We have the picture now of a powerful, well-financed, intelligently controlled quasi-religious movement which denies the very first article of our divine faith, which is avowedly non-Christian,— indeed anti-Christian,—in its policies and concepts, yet which strives to integrate with orthodox Christianity through an ecclesiastical sham which evokes all the sound and fury without any of the substance.

Unitarian-Universalists! Spot anything significant about the nomenclature? Humanists conduct their thinking upon a global or universal scale, — and to this end they are dedicated to unity, —

especially any type of unity which tends to bring everything under their own control.

Church unity, — the ecumenical crusade, — has been in vogue for many years now, and to the exclusion of more essential things, has become an obsession of church committees all the way from the Shetland Isles to Lizard Point, from the Nantucket Light to the beaches of California. Honest-to-goodness Catholics, Anglicans, Methodists, Baptists and Presbyterians, leading relatively blameless lives, worshipping tolerantly and devoutly as their fathers had done before them, suddenly made to feel that their faith and their way of life have somehow become inadequate! Parsons, priests and ministers, many of whom had assumed from the beginning that they were ordained into a Holy Christian Brotherhood encompassing all sects and denominations, and who had therefore come to perform their parochial duties entirely without animosity or prejudice towards any man, stricken with a guilt complex because their separate rituals and observances stood in the way of unification! The ideal of a World Super Church portrayed as God's ultimate will for the salvation of His children on Earth! Bibles, prayer books, hymnaries and holy ordinances scoured assiduously for elimination of sectarian doctrine or too fervent belief in the drive towards a lowest common denominator that would enable the whole of Christendom to cluster under a single banner! *To conform* being subtly given a more favoured connotation than to believe!

Why? Was it something that had been ordained from on high? After nearly two thousand years of diverse, fiercely cherished forms of worship, had the Lord suddenly decided that He was in the merger business, like a multinational corporation intent on trimming costs, cutting out incidentals, improving product presentation and rationalising sales in a social and economic climate dominated by the doctrine of survival? In other words, were the needs and pressures of church unification spiritual or secular? Did its high priests, its promoters, commune with the Almighty from time to time in heartfelt prayer, so that they could continuously be assured of divine guidance as they pursued their ecumenical mission? Or was Christianity just like any other commodity in the Space Age, up for grabs to anyone who could market it internationally in a globally attractive package?

¶ 23 INSTIGATING THE GLOBAL CHURCH

It was of course the humanists who first introduced the global dimension into our ecumenical palaverings. In their 1973 Manifesto they stated that "only a shared world and *global* measures will suffice", — and as they develop their concept of a world community and "system of world law and world order based upon transnational federal government", it becomes plain that religion is also scheduled for globalisation.

Away back in 1956 the Unitarians and the Universalists initiated the process when they merged to form the Unitarian-Universalist Church under the benign supervision of the American Humanist Association. Having set the ball rolling, they probably know better than most how to control it, — and if the ecumenical movement ever gets under way, with parishes and congregations, dioceses and patriarchates casting aside their sectarian doctrines and their inhibitions as they gleefully jostle their way through the crowded portals of that one super-church, who will they expect to find previously installed in the nave, or in the overflow assembly rooms, ready to dispense food and drink and other creature comforts to the furthest travelled of the pilgrims? Will it not be those selfsame Unitarians and Universalists, long convinced themselves of the necessity for unity and global measures, and conveniently devoid of any spiritual beliefs or attachments which would inhibit their patronage of a universal church common to people of all faiths and no faith at all?

¶ 24 ECCLESIASTICAL ASSET-STRIPPERS

That's it! Finally the truth is out. Friend! Fellow Christian! If you are one of those who have followed us through the traumatic twists and contradictions of "The Mind Benders" and "The Lemming Folk", you will readily appreciate that here is another occasion when conventional norms and axioms are about to be stood on their heads.

For the simple fact is that the movement for Christian unity has been inspired, orchestrated and master-minded by organisations and pressure groups *which are not Christian at all.* Their dynamism springs from the Humanist Associations of Britain and America and they have as much concern for our institutions and values as an asset-stripper spiriting away the disposables from a captive subsidiary before the inevitable liquidation.

It's hard to take it in all at once, — especially if this is something of which you have had no previous warning. That the Holy Christian Church could be infiltrated and threatened with ultimate takeover by a hedonistic and materialistic philosophy which denies the fundamental tenets of our faith! You have read about such nightmarish eventualities in the prophetic patches of the Bible, but somehow it never seemed to have any relevance to the present day. The local parson, priest or minister is such a good man, thoroughly devoted to the spiritual needs of his flock, — and as he preaches from the pulpit of a Sunday morning, his prayers and his sermons flow right from the heart. So how could *he* become party to such a monstrous deception, such an overwhelming betrayal of the fervent millions who try to model their lives upon the teachings of Jesus Christ?

Well how could he? And if he is aware of what is happening, why doesn't he speak out?

You realise of course that there must be more to it than that. When the argument is put in such crude terms, there may be few clergymen at the parish priest or village pastor level who will accept that their interpretation of divine doctrine has been compromised by humanism. Yet we have to ask ourselves whether a Church which had remained rock-solid in its fundamental beliefs and principles would ever have allowed itself to be deceived, even for an instant, by the fraudulence of an ecumenical movement which is strong on organisation, but distinctly neutralist in matters of faith.

So we've come to another stage, haven't we? a stage where, for a little while at least, we might profitably study the extent to which the Church is being threatened, not by outside influences, but by a reappraisal and a questioning of its divine mission from within.

CHAPTER IV

¶ 25 COMMUNISTS WITHIN THE FOLD

At the end of the Second World War there were few people in the United Kingdom who had not heard of Dr. Hewlett Johnson, the Red Dean of Canterbury, who shocked and scandalised the English Anglicans of his day by his heretical pronouncements and close identification with Communism, — yet who seemed sufficiently protected within the hierarchy to go on flaunting his revolutionary sympathies with complete impunity. Baron von Manhattan, a writer who specialises in a study of the Vatican, relates from time to time the efforts being made by powerful elements within the Second Vatican Council to install a Marxist pope. And in the later stages of this volume it is described how the groundwork for the Sandinista conquest of Nicaragua was laid by Jesuit priests who taught Communist philosophy and social subversion to the sons of middle-class families there.

It is not new. We have been living with it for some time now. The best service that we can render to ourselves, and to the society that sustains us, is to recognise the situation and expose it, so that one day the unbelievers may be thrown out of the temple.

¶ 26 IMPOSTORS IN DIVINITY

It appears that humanists have never been reluctant to join Christian churches, even when it meant making confessions of faith that were utterly in conflict with their own non-theist materialistic creed. Many must have felt sufficiently dedicated to present themselves for theological degrees, so that they might ultimately be ordained as priests and ministers in established churches, where their adherence to custom and their community relations would be above criticism, but where also they would be a numbing and a disastrous influence in those moments of crisis when only a true man of God would rise to the occasion, and provide hope and inspiration for those around him.

Humanist clergymen have worked assiduously to control the various administrative structures of church government, and to be the conveniently situated mouthpieces of ecclesiastical opinion. They provide most of the action in the ecumenical committees, and they pack the delegations that go off from time to time to conferences of the World Council of Churches in Geneva.

So how did it all begin? With some slipshod Professor of Divinity who allowed those bright-eyed humanist pioneers to graduate through his faculty without discovering that they were spiritually bereft, and virtual impostors? With obsessive theologians burning for an answer to the eternal questions of Creation and Resurrection, and getting themselves trapped in scientific arguments with the disciples of Darwinism? With the passage of time, and the erosion of simple faith as an element of divinity study, professorships coming to be filled by religious humanists themselves, so that it might be the devout and earnest student who faced an uphill struggle as he clung to his faith and his principles in face of adverse criticism? Christianity under the microscope, subjected to clinical methods of interpretation and deduction, and found wanting because no one could prove the virgin birth or the miracle of the five loaves and the two fishes?

¶ 27 THE SOCIAL GOSPELLERS

The Humanist Manifesto of 1973 had staked a powerful claim for cooperation on humanitarian grounds as it declared its objectives of controlling the environment, reducing disease, extending the life span, investigating and eradicating the cause of world poverty. It was a challenge which few churchmen could ignore or turn aside. Even those secure enough in their orthodox beliefs not to have any truck with the Manifesto, were yet obliged to admit that many of its aims were highly desirable, and that Christians ought to give their support to such reformist measures as were deemed practicable.

Perhaps too, in the climate of the times, and lacking any guidance to the contrary, many a priest and pastor quietly renounced his vows and embraced the new social philosophy, believing in the confident Manifesto prediction that it was destined to become the religion of the future. Compared with technology's modern miracles, Christianity might just have seemed a bit old-hat and riddled with primitive superstition. It wasn't as if they would require to make any drastic changes. For there was no reason why church worship should not continue as a social and a family habit, without a persistent raking after those spiritual values which could be so embarrassing when they carried less conviction than of yore.

Certainly, what with one thing and another, we had been ushered into the age of the social gospellers, the swinging folk-singing pastors who brought the pop sound into the choir chancel, and searched in the scriptures for dialogues with Marxism. And as an interesting statistic from the United States, Claire Chambers relates how in an issue of *Newsweek* dated June 26th 1967, a survey of the religious views of leading clergymen in the National Council of Churches revealed that only sixty per cent of them believed in the divinity of Christ and the promise of a life after death. That was the extent to which those churches had been taken over by the new creed of religious humanism.

¶ 28 NO LONGER ANYTHING SACRED

If at this stage you are mentally drawing a line between *religious* and *secular* humanism, be wary! For the humanists have already gone one step ahead of you. They say in Clause Seven of the 1933 Manifesto that "the distinction between the sacred and the secular can no longer be maintained".

Just what does that mean? That there should be a blurring and a fusion between that which is holy and ecclesiastical and that which is worldly and profane? The Church descending from its cathedral spires and entering into the market place? The Church on the hustings and in the social sciences! And by way of reciprocation, the local bookmaker or the stockbroker setting up their stands in the vestry! "Render unto Caesar that which *is* Caesar's," said the Lord Jesus Christ. But the modern day Pharisees would be troubled by no such distinctions, — and there were some old scores still to be paid off after His throwing of the moneylenders out of the Temple.

¶ 29 JAZZING IT UP AT THE GLIDE MEMORIAL

So the humanists were in on the ecclesiastical scene in a very big way. They had not broadcast their intentions with banner headlines in the national dailies, or on the prime listening and viewing spots of radio and television. But neither had they been particularly secretive with their own initiates, or with any outside party who was sufficiently interested to seek out the information. Humanism was in business as a religion. It was the religion which, in their own considered opinion, was destined to involve, encompass and ultimately absorb all other religions. As claimed in the 1973 Manifesto, it was to be the religion of the twenty-first century, the credo based on technical knowledge and reason which would best fit mankind for his conquest of the stars.

Compared with the breathtaking sophistication and scope of this latter-day Anti-Christ, the earlier assaults upon the Christian Church could only be regarded as a miserable failure. By burning down the churches and putting their priests and most earnest devotees to the sword, by banning all forms of organised worship and instituting draconian punishments against all who continued to profess spiritual beliefs, the atheistic ideologues of eighteenth century France and Bolshevik Russia merely kindled a flame in men's hearts which would not be extinguished until the churches were built again, and the faith was flourishing more strongly than ever.

By the subtlety and gradualness of their approach, the humanists would get most of their conquests on the cheap. Their new Universal Church would have little need for a sinking fund or a fabric fund, or any of the other administrative or financial requirements encountered by ecclesiastical management in other expansionist phases. What they wanted could always be acquired through infiltration, and assimilation of established structures of worship. Claire Chambers cites as an example of this the Glide Memorial United Methodist Church of the United States, which for the first two decades of its existence had functioned as a normal Christian organisation. But after the appointment of a humanist bishop in 1948 it changed its character entirely. Services became "celebrations", jazz groups took over the musical accompaniments from the traditional pipe organ, and the Bible was discarded in favour of a revolutionary booklet entitled *Quotations from Chairman Jesus,* —much of which had apparently been mugged from the recorded sayings of Mao-tse Tung.

When you learn also that one of its most prominent ministers in the nineteen-sixties had been identified as a member of the Communist World Peace Council, that he advocated free love and unrestrained living, ridiculed the concept of a heaven hereafter, permitted stripping, sexual intercourse and the screening of pornographic material around his altar, you realise that in some areas at least the humanist takeover was more of a smash-and-grab than an exercise in gentle persuasion. Such activities have apparently made the Glide Memorial a favoured rallying centre for revolutionaries and other subversives, and in 1969 a special "celebration" service was held to welcome the notorious atheist and Marxist activist Angela Davis. None of these well-publicised highjinks had prevented the Church's delegate from being a featured speaker at a United Methodist Conference in Atlanta during 1972.

This hilarious account of an American Methodist church totally taken over by humanism, appears in *The SIECUS Circle* (pages 299-302), a publication which naturally does not find its way on to every news stand, but which, if you can obtain it, makes very illuminating reading.

¶ 30 WORLD GOVERNMENT VIA THE WORLD CHURCH

Other successes for the *religious* humanists, especially in our own douce parishes and bishoprics, would be much less spectacular, but where they managed to capture the mind and soul of the pastor, they were well on the way to capturing a proportion of his flock, and down through the years cathedral and cloister, vestry and church aisle would start to ring out with humanistic concepts. So the new secular church would be built upon the stone and lime, the fabric and the furnishings, the donations and the endowments of the old, — and the parishioners and the congregations would not be any the wiser.

It was all to happen for the very best of reasons. Those religious humanists *believed* all right, — but not in an Almighty God. They believed in their own technologically-backed and intellectually cultivated cleverness, in the increasing ability of twentieth-century man to cope with his environment and probe the secrets of the Universe. They felt that their own philosophy was geared to take maximum advantage out of all such developments, and were utterly convinced that they and their elitist colleagues held in their hands the means by which all humanity could be uplifted into a more equitable and more secure future.

According to the 1973 Manifesto, they saw it as being within their powers to remove hunger, fear and discrimination from the face of the earth, to embrace all the diverse races of mankind within the jurisdiction of a single federal government, to merge all the religions and all the churches into one mighty super-church. In their own words, "Only a shared world and global measures would suffice."

So the parsons and the bishops, the ministers and the rabbis who were early in the queue to welcome the emergence of this new philosophy, and proudly to put their signatures upon its Manifesto, possibly did so with easy consciences and righteous hearts, believing themselves to be just that bit more far-seeing than their clerical colleagues, and that they were anticipating the trend and the consensus of the future.

¶ 31 FAITH AND THE GREAT CATHEDRALS

But here a nagging doubt emerges, — an element of caution obtrudes. Was it not rather sly and circumspect, — smacking of false pretences and fraudulent practices, — for those humanists and their ecclesiastical converts to engineer a clandestine takeover of the entire church establishment, with promises of such enhanced living and material progress as man had never previously seen, yet denying in their hearts the divine faith which is fundamental to all Christian doctrine? After all, the builders and the architects who cooperated to produce those monuments of stone, the craftsmen and the artists who laboured to form and ornament, the ordinary folk who gave of their time and their substance, the clergymen who ministered, and the parishioners who sanctified by their worship, all did so in the profound belief that they were working for the glory of God, Who would so respond to their efforts and their sacrifices that their lives would feel more fulfilled in consequence.

It is doubtful if they could have been spurred to such effort and sacrifice had they but known that their combined offering was ultimately scheduled to be taken over by a godless philosophy which professed neither respect for the Saviour nor belief in the life hereafter, — and all of whose future inspirations were to be derived from the carnal desires and mortal impulses of imperfect man.

¶ 32 A STRICTLY SECULAR VIEW

All right, let's come down out of the pulpit, and the gallery, and the organ loft for a minute, and talk to that wider bunch of secularists who couldn't care less one way or another, — whose own moments of dedication and reverence are centred round the football stadium or the wee white golf ball.

Stuff the cathedrals and the stained glass windows, you might say! O.k. for a gawk-about some holiday afternoon with the kids, or when you're acting as host to some American tourist with a penchant for the mediaeval! But beyond that the humanists can have them, — along with the panoply of mitre and crozier, the ceremony and the pageantry, the pious prayers and the sermonising, the hymn-singing and the bible classes, mothers' meetings, tea at the vicarage, and your best suit, shirt and tie of a Sunday morning. All part of the mumbo-jumbo of Christian myth-making and methodology down through the centuries!

Those stone masons, artists and artisans who created the cathedrals, — come to think on it, they must have been the world's greatest suckers! Creating monuments in stone which would be a wonder to generations then unborn, — and probably returning at night to shacks and hovels where they and their families dwelt in considerable squalor! Wouldn't catch you at it, would they, not unless they guaranteed premium rates with time and double time at the week-ends?

Would it not in fact have been more charitable to spare all the effort and munificence, and spread it around instead for the alleviation of the poor? Why take even the celebrated widow's mite for church-building, when there must have been so many more pressing causes for time and money and social involvement?

The answer is of course that we in this particular century don't have a choice. It was made for us before we were born. In the devotional fervour of that now distant age, the dignitaries of church and state, the priesthood, the burghers and the peasantry of township and hamlet, elected to spend a sizeable amount of their resources in the erection of those magnificent cathedrals which, with their architecture, their paintings and their carvings, have not been surpassed, even in our own richly endowed and technically advanced generation.

Let it be said again that they would not have brought forth such genius, such immensity of scope and conception, had they been asked to create a monument to humanism.

¶ 33 LETTING THE HUMANISTS HAVE A GO

But let's not drift too quickly away from our secular neighbours, colleagues and compatriots, now that we've got them thinking and talking. These guys have a fair amount of technical experience and expertise amongst them. They're used to making things function, — and function efficiently, — and are inclined to come down hard on anything that seems outdated, superfluous or irrelevant. So they'll judge the Christian Lord as they might judge a machine tool, or a works programme, or a proposed factory expansion. Do we need it? How will it affect our cash flow, our unit costs and our product presentation in the future?

No one could say that Jesus hasn't had His chance. Been on the go now for nigh on two thousand years, hasn't He? And some would argue, on strictly material grounds, that He hasn't made a particularly good job of it.

So why not let someone else have a go? If these humanists think they can control the environment, conquer poverty, reduce disease, expand the life-span and significantly modify human behaviour, — in fact perform all the miracles which have eluded bible-thumping churchmen down through the centuries, — why the heck shouldn't they have a go?

They certainly don't seem to be lacking in resources, ideas, education or technological achievement. A sagacious, erudite bunch on the whole! Stuffed with degrees and doctorates, fellowships and professorships! Principals of this college and that university! Egg-heads that *ought* to have the answers! So if they're determined to take over the churches, along with commerce and industry, and the global government of Planet Earth, why not just let them get on with it?

That, friends and fellow citizens, is the stage that has now been reached, — the stage where we let the humanists get on with it. At least for the time being, whilst we take a look at how their theories and their plans have been developing, not only in the churches, but in the secular world outside, — as they lay the groundwork for the humanistic revolution!

CHAPTER V

¶ 34 WORLD POPULATION CONTROL

Now it need occasion no surprise that in their long march towards a "shared world and global measures", the humanists would indulge in many apparent aberrations and digressions. They were not all of the same mind. They did not all put emphasis on the same things. And they appreciated the advantage of associations and alliances with kindred groups and ideologies which might help them some distance along the way. The original signatories to the 1973 Manifesto had signalled their identification with various other types of humanism, amongst which they specified the scientific, the ethical, the democratic and the Marxist. They held out a hand in greeting towards the free thinkers, the atheists, the sceptics and the agnostics. Humanists got themselves elected to federal and government agencies, joined world peace councils, mind research groups, civic rights and civil liberties unions, as well as anything even remotely connected with ecology, conservation and the potential internationalisation of natural resources. They also seem to have invented the world population crisis, and created the World Population Control movement as a means of solving it.

At first glance it might seem difficult to imagine why a philosophy dedicated to an extension of the good life in a man-made materialist world should devote so much of its time and inspirational effort to controlling the number of people who dwell therein. Yet in the last thirty years there are few areas where the new *herrenvolk* have been more willing to commit their prestige, their big names and their moneybags. In the 1950's the Scottish humanist Sir John Boyd Orr (later Lord Boyd Orr) wrote and lectured incessantly about the starving millions who would die slow and lingering deaths if prompt and stringent measures were not taken to curb man's natural fecundity. In response to this and other pressures on both sides of the Atlantic, a Population Crisis Committee had been formed in the United States in 1965, and by 1968 they even had a President's Committee on Population and Family Planning, chaired by no less a person than John D. Rockefeller III, grandson of the legendary oil millionaire, and himself the author of a book upon the coming humanistic revolution.

Now could there possibly have been a more significant piece of name-dropping at such a stage in the narrative? For with John D. III as honorary chairman of the fabulously wealthy Rockefeller Foundation, it was safe to assume that where desirable projects were concerned, he and his fellow humanists would not stumble for lack of funds.

¶ 35 STERILISATION IN INDIAN VILLAGES

Even so, in the prosperous and rapidly expanding Western economies of the sixties and early seventies, "population crisis" talk would be about as relevant as hard tack and army biscuits for a man settling down to a roast beef dinner. The synthetic hysteria generated by Boyd Orr peaked into prominence, then died away. The mass hunger with which the cranky Scottish food expert had threatened us was never to develop, — for the simple reason that agricultural research and improved farming methods were always able to produce the extra food to cope with the extra demand. The sophisticated peoples of the developed world, with their rising living and social standards, had already begun to restrict the size of their families as the amenities of a better life meant that the average lower or middle class couple would tend to bring forth only that number of children they could reasonably expect to rear and educate.

So the natural ingenuity and technical competence of Western man in solving or adjusting to his problems seemed at first to nullify the efforts of the population planners in the United States and the status-symbol economies of Britain and Europe. They had some success, and indeed more relevance, in some of the famine-stricken and disease-ridden societies of the under-developed world, where starvation and excessive child-bearing were long established norms. One of the most highly publicised population control experiments was in the vast sub-continent of India, where Mrs. Indira Gandhi, scion of that Fabian-orientated family which had ruled almost continuously since the partition of 1947, set in motion a scheme of mass sterilisation which had as its objective a scaling down of the teeming millions who dwell in the Deccan plateau and the Ganges Delta. It was a sort of pilot project for the backroom boys of World People Control, and one can imagine with what interest and favour they watched the zealous efforts to persuade village swains and full-bosomed peasant maids that there were other things to life than procreation.

Eventually, when the Gandhi Administration grew impatient, reports got out that they were sterilising healthy young men against their will. At that stage the plan backfired. Even in India, with all its problems of overbreeding and under-nourishment, there could be fierce resentment against the doctrine of compulsion, and popular reaction on this one issue was strong enough to throw Mrs. Gandhi temporarily out of office.

¶ 36 THE PILL AND THE ABORTION BILL

All right! maybe you had a certain amount of sympathy with the population planners in their efforts to reduce overcrowding on the Indian sub-continent, where human fertility had vastly outspawned its resources. We have had constant reminders of such situations recurring in parts of Africa and South-East Asia, with famines in such farflung areas as Biafra, Uganda, Bengal, Laos and Kampuchea. Much of this human misery would be aggravated by war, conquest and various forms of ideological exploitation. But basically it would be the age-old problem of primitive communities whose fragile societies had always borne the strains of minimum living standards and excessive child-bearing, so that they readily collapse under natural cataclysm or man-made disaster.

Our roving Tv reporters have done a thorough job on this

particular syndrome, haven't they, as they bring back harrowing colour documentaries of distended stomachs, malformed limbs, and children who have become walking skeletons of skin and bone? It was all happening so very far away, a hemisphere from the commuter belts of London, Manchester, Los Angeles and Montreal, but the inference was that *you* were involved, that somehow you had a measure of personal responsibility for chronic malnutrition in the Congo or the Ganges Delta. So you reached for your cheque book and you paid your contribution to Oxfam or Famine Relief, or whatever other international agency was planning massive airlifts to the stricken areas. You also thought to yourself, perhaps, that there must be a limit to the number of people that our planet can sustain on a reasonable level of nutrition and comfort, — and that there must indeed be something to this business of world population control.

All of which no doubt gave a boost to the doomsters of unbridled growth in those prosperous lands with a high density of colour Tv and ready access to *The New Yorker, The London Times* and periodic issues of *The Humanist.* In Britain family planning clinics became a commonplace feature of the National Health Service, and in America there was vastly increased funding and publicity for organisations with names like *Planned Parenthood* and *Zero Population Growth Inc.* The message had gone out that money and favours would be bestowed upon all who could best promote the image of a *caring* citizen readily responsive to the new economics of scarcity and the exigencies of the "population crisis".

Now that we have an opportunity to look back, now that we can appreciate in retrospect the enormous resources that were being directed into this type of persuasion, is it at all surprising that during the sixties and seventies health authorities seemed vastly more concerned with the curtailing of life than with its expansion or fulfilment? Spurred on by horror stories of what natural fecundity could do to the whole human race, they searched for every legal and medical means to prevent it. Never before had there been such preoccupation with matters like abortion, contraception and euthanasia. In the sixties the drug industry produced the oral contraceptive or "birth" pill, and also in the sixties a Scottish Liberal M.P. called David Steel, — then a trendy young man almost constantly in tune with humanistic values, — persuaded the British House of Commons to make abortion available on demand within the United Kingdom. As a result there was a time when London became the abortion centre of Western Europe, and such was the reduction in socially unwanted births that adoption agencies started going out of business.

¶ 37 FALLING BIRTH RATES IN THE DEVELOPED WORLD

As the coloured Tv documentaries continued to remind us, it wasn't doing much for the problems of overbreeding and under-production in the unsophisticated societies of Africa and Asia, but it had started to achieve the target of "zero population growth" among the developed races of the industrialised West. In Britain the mid-seventies saw a dramatic and apparently unanticipated downturn in the number of children coming forward for primary schooling, so that teacher training colleges, which had previously diluted their intakes and lowered their educational standards with the object of getting more qualified staff into the classrooms, suddenly found that they were not needed. Likewise school-building programmes had to be cut back, and many a reasonably up-to-date primary establishment compulsorily retired, all because there was no longer a clatter of tiny feet to stamp and echo down its waiting corridors.

In Germany the number of births per family unit had fallen from 2.16 in 1966 to 1.36 in 1978, and on this basis a statistician has predicted that, given a continuing trend in the same direction, there will be no more than ten million Germans left in a hundred years time. Similar figures are being quoted for the rest of the developed world, whether it be in the United States or Canada, Japan, U.S.S.R. or Eastern Europe. Births are failing to keep pace with mortality amongst the technologically gifted races, whilst the primitive peoples, especially those with access to modern medical skills and life-saving techniques, are poised for a dramatic upsurge in numbers.

You may be inclined to argue that there are logical and natural causes for a declining population in mature societies where opportunities are limited by finite resources, and where the constant bogey of unemployment can have a restraining influence on other things than parenthood. But what about a thriving, rapidly growing and developing country like South Africa, where the ruling and technically superior white race had been forced into a policy of *apartheid* or *separateness* because they were losing out in the numbers game with the blacks, who looked to them for stability, security and a rising standard of living, and showed their appreciation of this benign stewardship by doubling their birth rate every ten or fifteen years? Would you not expect, under influence of the same logical and natural causes, that the white South African, imbued by his leadership responsibilities, no less by considerations of racial survival, would want to see his natal clinics and maternity hospitals regularly patronised and filled to capacity? Would you ever believe that the Afrikaaner, eternally hammered and persecuted by the United Nations and the entire international community for his obstinate refusal to liberalise internal race policies and hand over his administrative and political power to that burgeoning black majority, would still become a sucker for the U.N. promoted and Rockefeller financed programmes on planned parenthood and zero population growth?

¶ 38 RACIAL SUICIDE IN SOUTH AFRICA

Yet in a book entitled "Where Have All the Children Gone?", Edward S. Williams, a South African medical officer, points to a rapid decline in birth rate amongst the white population since the Government adopted a family planning programme in 1974. He claims that whereas the zero growth figure is about 2.1 children per family unit, — and whereas this had been comfortably exceeded by at least fifty per cent in all the years up to 1974, — it had dropped to 2.12 births by 1978, and by 1980 would have fallen to below the minimum replacement quota. He also cites figures from a Cape Town obstetrics department which indicates that in a space of four years black and coloured babies had increased by percentages of eighty and twenty respectively, whilst the corresponding figure for whites was a decline of thirty-six. He knew of two private medical practitioners, operating what he termed the new "destructive gynaecology", who between them had performed upwards of eighteen hundred sterilisations on otherwise healthy women over a period of two years. Throughout the country there are, he said, a total of 1,988 clinics, spending a budget of eighteen million rand, all for the purpose of persuading South Africans that they live in a potentially overcrowded world, and that the only decent and civilised thing for them to do is limit their capacity for reproduction.

To this guff the indigenous Bantu, who love large families, had obviously responded with the derisory Churchillian finger signal, but the Afrikaaner, like his Anglo-Saxon blood-brother in Europe and the Americas, had swallowed the bait of the world population controllers, hook, line and sinker. Incredibly the natural rulers and administrators of a still young and developing country, a breed who could ill afford to weaken themselves militarily, economically or least of all numerically, — whose survival and technological progressiveness was not for the benefit of themselves alone, — had embarked upon a policy of racial extinction in a pathetic desire to conform.

¶ 39 WOULD THEY TRY COMPULSION?

So the developed races, whether in America or Europe or Southern Africa, — the civilised and sophisticated races who traditionally and inevitably produce the highest proportion of creative thinkers, scientists, technologists and general *problem solvers,* — had opted for the "zero population growth" syndrome, which meant that their aggregate numbers would go into a progressive decline, whilst in the under-developed world, where in many cases the reproductive process is a way of life, improvements in health care and reductions in infant mortality might lead to a population explosion.

Thus a natural consequence of the World Population Control campaign must mean that the sphere of the *problem solvers* is contracting, whilst that of the potential *problem makers* continues to expand, — a sobering thought in this age of egalitarian philosophies which give such undue prominence to the counting of heads, — and so little to what may be inside them.

You must have wondered at times how we could manage to get excited over a few humanist cranks preaching population control, — especially when on the one occasion they tried compulsion, it was thrown out with disastrous results for the instigators. Now however we have seen the power of persuasion, — and all that houha about sterilisation, legalised abortion and euthanasia begins to fall into perspective.

It does seem generally that women have tended to treat the new abortion laws as a matter of convenience, something to be left alone or utilised at will. And nothing that has been presented thus far may be taken as a threat to family life as it has been lived down through the ages. Whether to have children, — or not to have children, — is a choice that remains entirely with the parents, — and all that legislation and medical science have done is to widen the choices available. By the transplanting of Fallopian tubes, a child — or even children — for the wife who might otherwise have gone through her life barren! A safe, legal and unstigmatised abortion for her sister, to whom the whole process might have become socially and emotionally undesirable!

What with this and women's lib., the female sex appeared to be getting the best of it both ways. And in seeming contradiction to the "population crisis" campaign being massively financed by the Rockefeller Foundation throughout the Western World, Western governments were still providing a subsidy to parenthood, either planned or unplanned, by means of a family allowance which from country to country varied only in its degree of generosity.

So when would the population control lark turn into a nasty big sinister plot? Perhaps if they tried compulsion again, — and managed to make it stick! But *would* they try compulsion again? and under what circumstances?

¶ 40 HUMANISM AMONG THE TOP PEOPLE

This is the point where we take our time, — and consider all aspects of the matter. First of all it's intriguing, isn't it, to have established an incontrovertible link between humanism and the multi-millionaire Rockefeller family, whose conspiratorial influences upon the power politics of our generation have been exposed at some length in both "The Mind Benders" and "The Lemming Folk". We move out of the narrow academic world of venerable old philosophers like Bertrand Russell and the sociological lunacies of Dr. Spock when we come upsides with a Rockefeller. As we have noted, John D. III was not only a passing patron of humanism, — he was a dedicated adherent to its philosophy and its principles. His book *The Second American Revolution* left no one in any doubt that he wanted a society ruled entirely by humanistic values, and he served enthusiastically along with known Communists and other questionably motivated ideologues on population control committees, whilst his Rockefeller Foundation provided both the finance and the *entree* into high places.

Yes, humanism had joined the Big Power game when it took in the Rockefellers. Other humanists who moved in the highest political and financial circles were Robert McNamara, Chairman of the World Bank, Arthur Goldberg, a former justice of the U.S. Supreme Court, and Cyrus Vance and Walter Mondale, Secretary of State and Vice President respectively to bible-toting Jimmy Carter, — whose re-born Christianity had not been in any way repelled at the prospect of self-confessed unbelievers pivoting on the pinnacles of power.

So down through those last twenty-five years, and certainly during the last decade, there have been prominent highly influential humanists in the United States cabinet, humanists in the Supreme Court, humanists at the World Bank, humanists dictating the policies and setting the standards at the unofficial Council on Foreign Relations, and in the fabulously wealthy Rockefeller family foundations, — humanists at every power centre and pressure point where decisions can be taken that might influence the lives of millions of Americans, as well as those of untold millions more, whose safety and freedom depends upon principled and courageous American leadership.

It is not an idle boast when they claim that their creed is destined to be the social philosophy and the religion of the twenty-first century.

¶ 41 EVEN IN THE WHITE HOUSE

Does it matter? Anyone claiming that these top-flight humanist politicians and financiers are not sane, conscientious and responsible people? Anyone willing to doubt their credentials and their respectability, — the reputation for good works and philanthropy which many of them may enjoy in their own social and environmental circles?

The prevailing impression is that no one seems to *mind* any longer that a humanist might just have succeeded to the office of President of the U.S.A. It's not as if he was a Commie or a Leftie, or something, — and in any case we're told with considerable relish in certain quarters that both Britain and America have ceased to be Christian societies. So what right would we have to complain at a humanist in the White House, — and another one at 10 Downing Street for that matter? Also, what difference would it make?

Do Christians know? Or do we have to emphasise it all over again, — this business about the two big totalitarian systems of Nazism and Communism having to wipe Christian belief right out of their ideological creeds before they could begin their campaigns of terror and repression, — and how this paganism, this total lack of acceptance of a Divine Being, or of a life hereafter, is the one essential factor that Nazism, Communism and humanism have had in common?

¶ 42 CONTRACEPTION THROUGH THE WATER SUPPLY

In the ultimate, would the humanists resort to repression and compulsion, — for instance to implement their policies with regard to population control? All we can say is that if they felt inclined to do so, there would be no ethical values to restrain them, — and in *The SIECUS Circle* Claire Chambers maintains that many humanists have mentally advanced to this stage of enforcement many years ago. She quotes a Dr. Melvin M. Ketchel of Tufts University as saying, "If the birth rate cannot be controlled by voluntary means, then it is, I believe, a necessary and proper function of government to take steps to reduce it . . . *Drugs should be developed which can be administered to a whole population to statistically reduce the number of children born.*"

Yes, that's what the doctor said, — or is alleged to have said. Or,—the allegation having been made public, — there is no record of his having denied it. It doesn't matter all that much, for there is already sufficient evidence from various sources to show that we have within our Western democratic societies a body of influential opinion which feels that it knows best what is good for us, and will sponsor even the meanest forms of innuendo, falsehood and fabrication to see that we get it.

In "The Lemming Folk" we cited the views of another solemn biologist named Paul Ehrlich, who wanted to introduce a sterilising substance into the water supply, and provide antidotes, — under government control, — for those who were being permitted to have children.

Now we're really getting into a "1984" situation, aren't we? Can you imagine a courting couple having to display their credentials to an official at the Town Hall, so that he can decide whether reproduction of their particular genes is socially or politically desirable? Little phials of contraceptive antidote formally handed over under signature to intending brides and young wives once their permits to conceive have been officially granted! Inevitably, corruption in local council offices, so that permits, — as well as antidotes, — become available at a price, and end up on the black market! Voluntary seclusion in the wilderness for determined would-be mothers drinking untreated well water to achieve an illegal pregnancy out of reach of the bureaucracy!

Laugh? Who ever heard anything more far-fetched and ridiculous? Yet Dr. Ehrlich himself should not have been inclined to treat the subject with unseemly levity, since he was then an honorary president of Zero Population Growth Incorporated.

¶ 43 SELECTIVE STATISTICS

It seemed that at least some of the humanists in the World Population Control movement were becoming quite obsessive and increasingly hysterical. A sterilising agent in the water supply? Really! Short of establishing a Big Brother authoritarian dictatorship, they were unlikely to get away with that one.

Yet they had very nearly *won* the right to doctor our public water supplies when in the nineteen-fifties they got public health authorities in both America and the United Kingdom to endorse their demand for artificial fluoridation. You know what that's all about, don't you?

Doping our tap water with sodium fluoride or hydrofluoro-silicic acid in a controlled solution of one part per million, on the assurance that this would have a beneficial effect on children's teeth!

Their campaign on this particular measure was so sustained, so well endowed and directed, so assiduously promoted by health departments and prestigious dental and medical professional associations, that thirty years later there were more than 100 million Americans drinking, cooking and watering their garden vegetables with water to which fluoride had been added, — and in the United Kingdom they had only been frustrated by the independent attitudes of many local councils and water authorities, backed up by an informed body of lay and medical opinion which channelled itself through organisations like the National Pure Water Association and the National Anti-Fluoridation Campaign.

What? You hadn't previously thought of the humanists in this connection? You had been content to lay the blame for the fluoridation fraud upon the smelter industries and international chemical combines with their vast accumulation of fluoride waste products, — or the confectioners, sugar refiners and soft drinks manufacturers, with their vested interest in anything which purported to reduce tooth decay without clobbering the market for refined carbohydrates.

Fluoride promised to do just that. Ten years after the early experiments started in New York State towards the end of the Second World War, analysts were claiming that schoolchildren in the fluoridated city of Newburgh had sixty per cent fewer tooth cavities than were being recorded in the nearby city of Kingston, whose water supply had not been treated. They were not quite so optimistic in the Scottish town of Kilmarnock,where, when the experiment was terminated after five years, the improvement was reckoned in terms of two-thirds of a tooth per child. As statisticians pointed out, however, it was still possible to get figures that showed the sixty per cent advantage if you were sufficiently motivated. The trick was to concentrate your attention on the three-year-olds, because one of the known and well-recognised effects of fluoride is that it delays eruption of a child's milk teeth, and in the tender years youngsters reared on fluoridated supplies would have that much less time to develop dental caries than their contemporaries in the untreated control zones.

Like all good sales promotional aids, it was a bit of a gimmick, since findings taken progressively up the age scale were much less impressive. But it did help to sell the product, and at one time in the United States, city, borough and county councils were falling over themselves in their haste to establish fluoridation plants. Smelter and chemical industries benefited enormously. In one issue of *Chemical Weekly* a reporter stated that "the mind boggled" at the profits to be made by member companies from the remunerative unloading of their corrosive fluoride wastes, which were normally expensive to dispose of.

¶ 44 FROM POISON TO ESSENTIAL NUTRIENT

So far so good! Good for the smelting and chemical conglomerates, who were enjoying a boost in turnover! Good for the sugar refiners, the fizzy drink bottlers and the toffee-makers, who could argue that their sweet and sticky confections would not be responsible for rotting the teeth of the next generation if only the guardians of the public water supplies could be persuaded to go for fluoride! Good for the consciences of the city fathers, who had been made to feel that they stood at an epic milestone in man's forward progress, as they legislated for the abolition of the toothache!

Within the American bureaucracy, too, standards were subtly changing. The Food and Drug Administration, which had always classified fluorides as poisons and banned their use as food additives,— and which moreover had previously studied ways and means of getting naturally occurring fluorides out of the water supply — now categorised fluorine's compounds as nutrients essential to life, and in 1974 there was a court decision instructing the F.D.A. to issue regulations for its addition to general purpose foods, as well as guidance for its use as a dietary supplement. Advocates of fluoridation on both sides of the Atlantic promptly took up the cue, and started talking in terms of *correcting a fluoride deficiency.*

¶ 45 SAFE — PROBABLY SAFE, — WELL, MAYBE!

Now does that not make you just that teeny bit suspicious, — especially those Christian folks who have always believed that the

Good Lord's natural environment is entirely adequate for a healthy and a satisfying life? Had there for instance been a fault at the time of the Creation, when it had been left to the biologists and biochemists of the Second Millennium A.D. to compensate for the erratic distribution of a nutritious substance which man could ill do without?

The American F.D.A. was in two minds about this. It wanted to accept the court's ruling, but it was still reluctant to classify fluoride as a safe food additive, — bearing in mind that one of the commonest fluorine compounds is a well-known rat poison. For a while those scientific and dedicated watchdogs of the American diet continued to list fluoride as an "essential". By 1976, however, it had been downgraded to "probably essential", and by 1979 they obviously felt in their wisdom that it was best to drop the idea altogether. Fluoride once more became "not generally recognised as safe", — which is a bit of a mind bender in view of the fact that health boards up and down the country are still stridently demanding its wholesale use in the public water supply. After all, you might argue, if it's poison when eaten with a knife and fork, surely it's just as much a poison when swilled over in a glass of water or blended into a pint of beer.

Not so, say those big-hearted, caring and compassionate fluoridators! This is one occasion where a little bit of poison does you good. Provided through the public water supply, it can be measured in a carefully controlled solution, — to a recommended level of one part per million in fact, — and at that level we have a guarantee from the Minister of Health, the Royal College of Physicians, the British and American Dental Associations and a whole army of highly qualified academic luminaries as to its complete and utter safety.

¶ 46 THE ANNAPOLIS OVERSPILL

All right! but what happens in the event of an accident? Even at a proportion of one part per million, considering the gallonage passing through some of the larger fluoridation plants, there had to be lethal quantities of toxic chemicals stored within easy access of the system. Suppose something went wrong!

Well, on November 11th, 1979, in the American city of Annapolis, something did go wrong. A public works employee opened a valve on a large tank of hydrofluoro-silicic acid, and forgot to turn it off again. Before the mistake was discovered, an excess thousand gallons of the corrosive chemical had been spilled into the city's water supply. The supervisor to whom the mishap was ultimately reported decided on a cover-up, and details of the accident were not made public until health officials started investigating a sudden deterioration in the condition of eight kidney patients who had been on dialysis in the days following the overspill. Other consequences were the death of one elderly man by cardiac arrest, the wiping out of fish stocks in the local aquariums, and the mandatory destruction of thousands of cases of soft drinks which had been bottled whilst the water supplies were heavily contaminated.

Local health officials in Annapolis had refrained from warning the public about the accident for fear that it would jeopardise their fluoridation programme.

¶ 47 THE SAD CASE OF LITTLE WILLIAM KENNEDY

So when is "safe" completely safe? And how many other ways are there of getting a toxic overdose if the authorities persist in putting fluoride into our tap water? Unlike chlorine or methane, fluorides cannot be boiled out of solution. Indeed in conditions of high evaporation they must inevitably concentrate, so in a fluoridated area the housewife who nearly boils the kettle dry before making a pot of tea is liable to poison herself and any associated members of the family. Likewise with over-cooked meats and vegetables! The water flies off in the form of steam, — the fluoride concentrates itself in the food matter that's left.

What about fluoride mouth washes and dentifrices, the latter of which provide the subject for so many seductive and compelling television adverts? You know the drill! Brushing with so-and-so's toothpaste plus MFP fluoride means fewer and fewer fillings! But kids are known to swallow toothpaste by the brushload, — especially if it's got an attractive minted flavour. They're getting a double dose, aren't they, if they're also brushing with fluoridated water?

As for fluoride mouth washes, — well on 19th January 1979 a New York jury awarded 750,000 dollars in damages to a Mr. and Mrs. Clay Kennedy for the utterly pathetic death of their three-year-old son, killed by a lethal dose of fluoride administered to him at a dental clinic in Brooklyn. During a routine mouth examination a hygienist spread a 2% solution of stannous fluoride over the boy's teeth before giving him a cup of water with which to rinse out. The youngster unwittingly swallowed the water, and along with it a triple overdose of the highly toxic stannous fluoride. He died in an adjacent hospital a few hours later.

¶ 48 FLUORIDATORS CAUGHT IN COLLUSION

The case history against human ingestion of fluorides was steadily and inexorably accumulating. Having finally overcome their apprehension of the dental and medical establishments hooked on fluoridation, doctors and dentists were coming forward with studies and observations of their own. Nutritionists and food chemists started to publish findings about the amounts of fluoride involuntarily ingested in such common food and beverages as fish and tea, and the hypothesis that any one individual's total intake of the fluorine ion could possibly be controlled by doctors or local authorities or water engineers, looked more and more ridiculous. The Burk-Yiamouyiannis cancer statistics, ferociously attacked by the National Cancer Institute in America and the Royal College of Physicians in Britain on grounds that they had not been corrected for age, race and sex, had been thoroughly vindicated in two courts of law, and their detractors forced to confess under oath that they had been guilty of collusion and misrepresentation. Under one exposure after another, totally deprived of any fresh research or newly assembled data which might add conviction or encouragement to their point of view, the protagonists of artificial fluoridation lashed about them in an ever-decreasing circle, frantically seeking endorsements each from the other, and all the time proclaiming that the measure was safe because they, the elite of their profession, had declared it to be safe.

¶ 49 THE CAMPAIGN THAT WENT ON REGARDLESS

But they were really on a hiding to nothing. Or weren't they? The great fluoride hoax had had a truly spectacular run, but an alerted public in both Britain and the U.S.A. had finally tumbled to the con. trick, and it was only a matter of time before the dental and medical associations, the ministries and the health boards quietly dropped the subject from their agendas, and blandly went their way as though it had all been an exercise in public relations. The fallacy of a panacea for tooth decay was destined to follow the concept of a wonder drug for painless child-bearing, and the mediaeval practice of bleeding patients suffering from anaemia.

Strictly on the evidence, this is what one might expect to happen —ethically attuned professional bodies realising that they had been manoeuvred into a blind alley or a wrong turning, and promptly taking remedial action to get themselves back on the road! Ministries and health officials responding to public concern, and amending or discontinuing experiments which did not have popular support! Local councils being allowed to discuss and dismiss the matter once and for all, instead of being persistently petitioned, advised and directed, inveigled by central government grants and indemnities into just one more attempt at putting over fluoridation on a reluctant and suspicious electorate!

So why had things not been allowed to take their natural course? Why had the punch-drunk boxer, saved by the bell and staggering into his corner on the count of nine, not been allowed to slump in his seat and throw in the towel, rather than being pumped full of stimulants which would send him back into the centre of the ring swaggering with bellicosity and a new-found bravado?

¶ 50 MEDICAL ETHICS TAKE A BACK SEAT

During the fluoride debate, it was the proponent doctors and dentists who would provide the most obvious clue. With the downgrading of the Christian ethic, and amidst a conflict of personal and psychological pressures, too often there was a tendency to fudge the answer to a medical or clinical problem, — to come up with conclusions that some influential sponsor or pressure group was demanding, — rather than what might prove to be an unpalatable truth.

In the protracted controversy which followed publication of the Burk-Yiamouyiannis statistics on a link between cancer and fluoridation of water supplies, certain celebrated members of the British medical establishment were caught in an untypical and thoroughly unethical manoeuvre.

Prompted by Dr. Hoover of the American National Cancer Institute into an instant rebuttal of the Burk-Yiamouyiannis figures, which threatened to destroy the fluoridationist case entirely, two specialists Sir Richard Doll and Dr. Leo Kinlen accepted the N.C.I. information and published it in "The Lancet" as data which they themselves had compiled from open sources. Kinlen then passed on the Hoover computations to Professors Oldham and Newell of the Royal Statistical Society, and hinted that it might help if they could be seen to produce an independent opinion. Oldham and Newell then published the data under their own names in the journal "Applied Statistics".

The trouble was that there had been a certifiable error in the Hoover statistics, and this same error had been compounded in both the Doll-Kinlen submission and that produced by the statisticians Oldham and Newell. At a court in Pittsburg, Pennsylvania, in front of Judge J. Flaherty, Dr. Kinlen was subsequently obliged to admit under oath that there had been collusion in the compilation of the data which purported to demolish the Burk-Yiamouyiannis cancer link, and three years later, at the Court of Session in Edinburgh, Professor Newell admitted likewise that he had *not* made an independent examination of the cancer-link figures, so that his unqualified endorsement of the Kinlen-Doll and Hoover computations had been wilfully misleading,—might indeed, had it been allowed to prevail, have denied both British and American citizenry the benefit of a valid enquiry into the cause of waterborne cancer.

¶ 51 POPULATION CONTROL AGAIN

This was not what you and I had come to expect of our medical and professional dignitaries, — such a complete lack of clinical detachment, —such a scrubbing around to make the facts fit the hypothesis, rather than that uncompromising search after truth which is the precious element in all original research and discovery.

So after that rigorously contested but still uninvalidated cancer scare; after the Annapolis overspill, with its implied warning that it could happen again at any time whilst fluoridation was in progress;

after the clearly established threat to the lives of cardiac patients and kidney sufferers, whose weakened constitutions are unable to withstand surges in the ingestion of fluorides; after the harrowing story of three-year-old William Kennedy, who died after swallowing a fluoride mouth wash; after an avalanche of well-documented research on allergies, diabetes, skeletal deformities and the progressive identification of more and more forms of fluoride toxicity; after all this, just what was it that kept the fluoridation bandwaggon rolling?

We can assume that the smelter industries and the chemical combines who create the fluoride wastes would still be riding shotgun, since there's a pot of gold waiting for those swashbuckling *hombres* at the end of the day if the waggon train should reach its caravanserai intact. The confectioners and the soft drink salesmen could still be tagging on hopefully down the trail, keeping sweet with the waggonmasters and knowing that there's an advantage for them too, in the shape of protected profits, if tooth decay can ever be successfully diagnosed as a fluoride deficiency rather than a misuse of carbohydrates.

Ethical-minded doctors and dentists, straight-thinking scientists and dieticians, all manner of principled and altruistically motivated researchers and administrators, have jumped trail long ago and headed for the opposite horizon. The only honest-to-goodness folks still crewing the waggons and helping to keep things rolling, are those who have never really bothered to find out what is happening. Up front the big trail bosses, calling the shots, keeping their own counsel, — never ever revealing what might be their ultimate destination!

But by this time you and I have *some* idea, haven't we? We realise that there is only one materialistic philosophy with enough financial muscle, influence over the mass communications networks, infiltration in depth into central and federal government bureaucracies, — to fly in the face of documented research, commonsense and popular antagonism, and just keep on rolling towards its self-ordained objective, regardless of who or what might be sacrificed in consequence.

Yes, you've guessed it! It's back to those humanist giants of the World Population Control movement. Drugs for administering to entire nations and regions within those nations, *so as to statistically reduce the number of children born!* Sterilising agents introduced into the water supply, — with antidotes provided at government expense for those permitted to have a family!

All far-fetched! All twenty-first century fantasia that might have been dreamed up by the purveyors of science fiction, or script writers to late-night television melodrama! But how much easier it might be to implement if by then the would-be fluoridators had won the right to medicate your tap water on the basis that it would improve the children's teeth!

CHAPTER VI

¶ 52 HUMANISTS AND FABIANS

In "The Mind Benders" we described at some length how the early Fabians had invented the social sciences so that they could mould the English educational system into a tool of the Gradual Revolution. We are now about to investigate what effects the humanist revolution has had upon that much-tried and once admirable educational system. So the next and most obvious question to be answered is: what are the differences between Fabianism and humanism? and what are their varying approaches to education?

First, let's try some definitions. The Fabians got their name from the Fabian Society, founded in 1883 by a group of nineteenth century English socialists, initially under the sponsorship of Edward Pease, but subsequently to be guided by Sidney and Beatrice Webb and the literary giant George Bernard Shaw. They were not definitively atheistic or anti-Christian, though many of their early writings betrayed an irreverent and a questioning attitude to things spiritual. They proposed to change society by a policy of gradualness, and their ultimate aim was socialist revolution.

The humanists can fairly be described, from their two manifestos, as a homogeneous group of twentieth century sophisticates whose common bond of association is their total rejection of spiritual values and of all forms of divine guidance. The fact that many humanists, for tactical purposes, dissemble before the Christian world and engage in pseudo-religious observance, is quite immaterial, — the driving force of their movement is anti-religion and anti-God. Like the Fabians, humanists also have plans for changing society, — they include phasing out nations and nationalities, and bringing all humanity under a single authoritarian government.

So where does Fabianism end and humanism begin? And to what extent are the personalities and the aims and principles interchangeable? Are most Fabians nowadays also humanists? And if they are, can we describe them as Fabian-humanists or humanistic Fabians?

Also, can the converse be equally true? Do our modern generation of high-powered and well-heeled humanists subscribe to the socialist ambitions and Gradualist Revolutionary aims of the Webbs and their present day disciples in the newly formed Social Democratic Party?

Friend, in this company it's futile to split hairs. You may occasionally get some uppity Fabian who tells you he's a socialist because he reads his bible, — or a humanist millionaire who gets a bit equivocal about egalitarian concepts on account of what it might do to his dividends. But for Christians and conservatives, — for all in whatever rank or station who love freedom of thought and action and the spirituality of the individual soul, they are both very bad medicine, and for all practical and ideological purposes can be grouped together.

¶ 53 INDOCTRINATION VIA THE SOCIAL SCIENCES

Now! we were talking about education, — specifically, the instruction and guidance of our children, the development of their minds and fulfilment of their latent talents and ambitions, so that they will grow up as useful citizens, trained and ready to carry on the society which we shall eventually give into their hands. Our previous study of Fabianism in "The Mind Benders" had illustrated how keen were those early Fabians on education, — how they had seen the necessity for indoctrinating the young if they were ever to bring their ideas of social change into being. A fundamental step in that programme was the "creation" of the social sciences, — new and previously unconsidered studies such as psychiatry and sociology, where almost everything was subject to interpretation, and there were few irrefutable facts to interrupt the progress of social engineering.

Application of Fabian theories, influencing of the young untutored mind for purposes of political orientation rather than imparting instruction and stimulating the imagination, was a gross breach of the trust which parents repose on teachers when they allow them to have complete charge of their children in the guarded seclusion of the classroom. But Fabian educators had salved their consciences on that point, and had gone a long way in the consolidation of their new social philosophy before the proclamation of the First Humanist Manifesto.

¶ 54 HATE OBSESSIONS THAT PERVERT THE YOUNG

It is probably an impossible ideal to try and keep all political bias out of the classroom. Even the old traditionalist custom of instilling the young with a healthy respect for God, Queen and Country might be interpreted by a Marxist Republicanist as unfairly prejudicing a generation of youthful citizens against the philosophy which he himself regards as best befitting the future. The Marxists themselves have of course been totally unscrupulous in their abuse of college and schoolroom to promote the concepts of class revolution, and where they have managed to create Marxist-socialist enclaves, as at the notorious William Tyndale School in the nineteen-seventies, have orientated the entire curriculum away from academic instruction and towards forthright political indoctrination.

A counterblast to this has been the distribution round English primary schools of propaganda stirring up feeling against coloured or ethnic minority groups, and urging confrontation with the radicals of the Left lunatic fringe. Kids who come under these influences beat up black and Asian youngsters, smear paint and slogans on the front doors of undesirable aliens, and are persuaded to blame all their ills, from a tummyache to social deprivation, upon their unfortunate neighbourhood Jews. When they get older, these young people, if nurtured on the same undiluted doctrines, will aspire to bloody street clashes with the Young Socialist League, the Trotskyists, the Anti-Nazis and whatever other ideological diversion the exponents of class revolution will dream up to sustain the politics of confrontation. All good robust bigotry, and all devoted to a denial of the precious right to an unbiased, liberal education!

¶ 55 CORRUPTING THE UPPER CRUST

Fabian subversion, as directed by the Webbs in Britain, and instituted in the United States by the likes of John Dewey, was inclined to be disseminated from the top downwards. Because the Fabians were an elite, and intended to remain as such, their early converts were in England's classiest universities and public schools,—

that Oxford Union vote against defence of King and Country was a dramatic tribute to their initial penetrations. As we have seen too, the "progressive" teaching methods introduced by John Dewey at the Lincoln School of Columbia University were also successful in corrupting the third generation of multi-millionaire Rockefellers, with calamitous results for a Western World threatened by Communist domination.

Essentially the Fabians went after the upper crust of society, — the footloose and under-motivated sons of noble families, the college dons and top academics of famous universities, the teachers and lecturers, the articulate and the urbane, — as well as the eccentric, the talented misfit, the envious, the pathetically inadequate and the supercilious, — all those who for one cause or another had reason to resent the established order of things. They were vastly successful in subverting the American Federal bureaucracy and the British Civil Service, particularly the Foreign Office, which would defy even the determined onslaughts of a Thatcher to thwart its obsession with internationalism. As noted in "The Lemming Folk", Fabian indoctrination inserted such treacherous Marxist scarecrows as Donald MacLean, Guy Burgess and Kim Philby into the British Diplomatic Service.

¶ 56 LIMITATIONS OF POLITICAL THUGGERY

But Fabian teachings and subversion, its arrogance, its elitism, its effeteness and its innuendos, had often appeared as no more than a crust upon the surface of the body social and politic. It was undoubtedly an upper crust, it affected the natural ruling and administrative class, it quickly moved into and dominated the corridors of power. But its demoralising doctrines were slower to disseminate through the class structure. Whilst the youthful Lord Fauntleroys and their over-privileged contemporaries at Eton and Cambridge were cowering under their guilt complexes and preparing to dismantle the British Empire, the sons and daughters of the lower middle-class were still getting a healthy patriotic education at state-assisted secondaries and grammar schools up and down the country. When they came to maturity, and moved into business or the professions, they would vote, remonstrate and fulminate against the seditious tendencies which were eroding their homeland's military and economic power base, — but without any prospect of changing the system, since the pinnacles of political and administrative power had already been captured by a self-perpetuating elite whose philosophy straddled the party system and made a total mockery of democratic selection.

It was as insidious as it was frustrating. Fabian predominance in politics, in the civil administration and in the mass communications industry had established a kind of ionised layer through which protest and alternative ideas were not allowed to penetrate. Radical and original thought came to an abrupt end whenever they threatened the established norms.

But still it was essentially superficial. Still there were people with hard and difficult jobs to do, people with years of practical experience behind them, people whose vast involvement in real life as it was lived, — rather than the doctrinaire world of the theorists, — had made them utterly distrustful of Fabian guff and legerdemain, people of heart, commonsense and honest-to-goodness patriotism, people of every class, occupation and level of education, who sensed what was going wrong with their society, and who resisted at every opportunity the effete and trivialist tendencies which were destroying the faith, confidence and enterprise of their nation.

As for those highly publicised sideshows, such as the National Front marches and the demonstrations and counter-demonstrations of the Trotskyists, the Young Socialists and the Anti-Nazi league, they might result in a few arrests and broken heads, local distress and social disruption, an increase of tension and an overspill of violence in sensitive areas, — but in the end they weren't going to *change* anything. Even the kids who had had their immature little heads filled with race-hate or anti-capitalist slogans, — such as the young monsters who terrorised ethnic minorities in England's Midland cities, or the Glasgow schoolchildren tutored into writing abusive essays about a Tory Prime Minister, — need only be taken out of the hands of their ideologically motivated mentors to gravitate into a more balanced view of politics and society.

Street violence had its limitations. Mature and responsible

Situation ethics, — smudging the dividing line between right and wrong

minds immediately dismissed it for what it was. Neither the N.F. propagandists nor the fanatical Marxists who subverted the children of the William Tyndale school were ever going to be allowed to create a generation of racist thugs or ideological paranoiacs. For it was all too crude, too sudden, — and too much against the British way of doing things.

¶ 57 AN INTRODUCTION TO SITUATION ETHICS

How now for the humanists? *They* also wanted to change things, —said so in their manifestos. Traditional moral codes and religious values had failed to meet the pressing needs of today and tomorrow, they argued, so by implication they were intent on creating a new code of ethics, new advanced moral standards which would fit mankind for moving into the twenty-first century.

Fuddy-duddy Christian orthodoxists might just be stuck with the old-fashioned impression that moral values were absolute, — which shows how far out-of-date they have become in an age that has to be prepared for global measures. The humanist answer was a novel conception which they called "situation ethics", and which was apparently one of those convenient innovations which can mean what you want them to mean.

Situation ethics is all about smudging the dividing lines between right and wrong. Under the traditional code of values, for instance, it was invariably wrong to lie or cheat, steal, calumniate or be disrespectful to one's elders and teachers. As judged by the new humanist code, these actions and attitudes would invariably be subject to qualification. Did a child steal because it felt deprived of the good things available to its playmates? Did it lie because a truthful confession would have earned a severe punishment? Did a youth commit some atrocious act of violence or vandalism to gratify some repressed instinct, — or to get his own back on a society which seemed indifferent to his problems? Did the class feel justified in dismissing their tutor as a stupid old windbag because the pontificating idiot failed to touch on those pursuits and interests which really turned them on?

Good and bad! Right and wrong! Wickedness and seemly virtue!

The humanist abhors such absolute terminology, and endeavours to rationalise human actions and motivation within a new scale of values where everything is relative. In *situation ethics* stealing could be interpreted as a desirable redistribution of property; mendacity as an imaginative reconstruction of the facts; violence as an expression of revolt against an unjust, uncaring society.

The real beauty of the new code is that judgment is devolved upon the individual. If little Johnny sees an opportunity to swipe the school dinner money, rough up the headmaster's study and pin the blame squarely on the teacher's pet, there's nothing in the code of situation ethics which rules that he should subsequently own up, come clean or endeavour to make restitution for his behaviour. In his own mind the fact that he was prompted to do what he did could become in itself a justification, — and though the humanist educator might *deplore* his anti-social tendencies, without absolutes it would no longer be possible to categorise his conduct in terms of right and wrong.

¶ 58 THE COLLAPSE OF EDUCATIONAL STANDARDS

While parents are still deliberating upon the effects of this quaint philosophy on a state school system which is seen to be failing the nation, let's focus on another aspect of the humanist revolution in education.

Barbara Morris, an American who has made a close study of humanistic teaching methods, emphasises that as a result of the new ideas, state schooling is no longer a process whereby the younger generation gets a thorough grounding in reading, writing and arithmetic, punctuated with tempting excursions into the higher planes of learning. Rather is it, she says, "a process of social change, creating humanistic citizens with a world view of life". Old-style academic instruction is now treated disparagingly as the imparting of "knowledge items", and is relegated to a minor place in the curriculum.

Well, what do you make of that? No wonder Sonny Boy cannot do the simplest of sums, or that daughter is graduating from high school with only the most rudimentary grasp of English grammar!

Not at all surprising that by 1981 Education Departments in the United Kingdom were considering the dropping of even the modest "O" level leaving certificates, and their substitution by a new *Foundation* standard which would be so rudimentary in its requirements as to be within reach of all!

¶ 59 AN INDICTMENT OF TRENDY TEACHING METHODS

There is a widely cultivated belief nowadays that education is all about spending money. In the years since the Second World War educational budgets have soared to the extent that they are now by far the largest single item listed in the expenditure of local authorities. Ensuring that the kids got a decent schooling became a priority with many thousands of working class families, and there was little resistance to the proportion of rates and taxes that was regularly allocated to this purpose. When the Thatcher Government, which came to power in May of 1979, started trimming back on education along with other forms of public spending, there were outraged cries from teachers' associations and Opposition politicians to the effect that such ill-considered economies would cripple the prospects of the next generation. Remarkably, no one bewailing the curtailment of educational budgets thought fit to note the fact that standards have been falling all through the years of lavish spending, — and no one, even amongst those responsible for the economy cuts, considered it worthy of mention that the rudiments of educational advancement are a teacher with a zest for imparting knowledge and a pupil eager to learn.

Certainly no one mentioned the humanist revolution. Yet that was having a far more fundamental effect on the attitudes and standards of the next generation than any trimming of educational budgets. For it must be obvious that in a humanised schools system where the traditional symbols of erudition are relegated to the status of "knowledge items", and where the main emphasis is upon "a process of social change creating humanistic citizens with a world view of life", there is bound to be a dramatic reduction in academic standards.

There is no disputing the fact that this has already happened.

Industrialists in Britain who regularly absorb an intake from the state schools for clerical and processing activities, have been complaining for years about the abysmal lack of rudimentary knowledge evinced by their applicants. Sixteen-year olds who stumble over the simplest arithmetical problems, and who have only the vaguest notions about spelling the commonest English words! who would sweat and swither over the composition of an elementary business letter, and whose awareness of the world about them is limited to the pop scene and the disc-cutting proclivities of the latest pelvis-wiggling wonder to make the Top Ten!

Yes the humanist revolution was stealthily achieving its objectives, — and in such a manner that no more than a fraction of the rates- and tax-paying public could have the faintest idea what it was all about. So what *was* it about? What logic could there be in an influential group of trendy educators so disrupting basic instruction as to bring forth a generation of academic morons? Could it be that those humanists, who have long-range ambitions towards the controlling of society, are concerned to see that the *hoi polloi,* for all their increasing affluence and improving living standards, should not get too smart?

The author does not provide glib and easy answers. He merely points to the facts, many of which are obvious enough, despite all the obfuscation and bland concealment. A post-war society which in both Britain and America was desperately anxious to achieve an educational breakthrough for its children, — which was both eager and willing to give generously of its tax revenues so that its offspring could enjoy expanding opportunities in an exciting technological future, — has somehow failed to maximise on its investment. A government school inspectorate which conducted an eighteen-month study of some 5,000 pupils in English primary schools, and which finally issued its findings in September of 1978, made a conclusive indictment of "trendy" teaching methods when it reported that children subjected to the new informal discovery techniques were far behind the traditionally trained in both reading and mathematics assessments. Best results had been achieved by teachers who stuck to formal instruction sessions, using blackboard and chalk, jotters and the working out of practical illustrations.

¶ 60 ENCOURAGEMENT FOR THE OLD SCHOOL

Bravo for the stodgy old "squares" of Her Majesty's School Inspectorate! They had put their fingers on the trendy devotees of futuristic education, and many of them must have wriggled uncomfortably under the scrutiny. They had also struck a mighty blow for good old-fashioned common sense, and given new hope to those hard-working classroom traditionalists who must often have wondered whether their skills and experience had truly become outmoded in a world of instant coffee, electronic communication and press button techniques of instruction.

Not that you and I can afford to be complacent as a result of this report! Old-fashioned and traditionalist-minded school inspectors eventually retire or die off. The next generation might themselves be composed of "trendies" unless we rumble what has been going on, and re-inculcate a respect for tried and tested values. For what else are those way-out informal *discovery* techniques and *trendy* discussion methods but a manifestation at classroom level of the humanist revolution, passed down by college theorists and progressivist educators who see the educational system as a "process of social change creating humanist citizens with a world view of life", and who would no doubt judge it a considerable success to produce a generation of students whose minds were uncluttered with "knowledge items", mathematics or English grammar?

¶ 61 ILLITERACY IN THE U.S.A.

Over in the United States, where things are always at least ten years ahead of anywhere else, President Jimmy Carter felt obliged in 1978 to pluck a forty-nine year old academic from the University of New York and appoint him as a Commissioner of Education in order to promote a "literacy" campaign, — this because it had been brought to his notice that *kids were graduating from college without being able to pass a basic test in reading, writing and arithmetic.* In "The Mind Benders" we quoted William J. Buckley, a well-known New York conservative who had once wrily remarked that the only way to save his country's educational system was to give every

American child a diploma when it was born, thus leaving room in the colleges for those with a genuine quest for knowledge. More recently, — as has been noted in a previous passage, — our own United Kingdom education departments were preparing to accommodate a drastic drop in academic values by scrapping the "O" levels and issuing a new *Foundation* certificate based on minimum standards which would be easily attainable by all.

Dr. Ernest Boyer, the man President Carter had appointed to promote his literacy campaign, felt that the way to solve the problem was to get back to *basic skills* and traditional teaching methods. Well! well! that's what the French would call *deja vu.* It seemed that even in the U.S.A. trendy humanist educators were having to beat a retreat as outraged parents got a sample of their philosophy, and what it could mean in wasted lives as ill-adapted youngsters were pushed into the streets fit only for social security handouts, and ready targets for the protest movements that thrived on social revolution.

CHAPTER VII

¶ 62 OBFUSCATING THE FAILURES

Satisfied that we've licked the humanists on the education front,—that it only needs a few more Presidential Commissions, vigilance by the H.M. School Inspectorate, a new commitment to basics and traditional teaching methods, — and the humanist educational experiment of the sixties and seventies will become a thing of the past?

Don't rely upon it. The trends and reports which we have mentioned are an encouraging look back to sanity, but they are still superficial. The alarming drop in academic standards throughout our state-run comprehensive schools has been related to the activities of college theorists and trendy educators, but it has not been related back publicly and officially to the humanists. Officialdom has threshed about, wondering aloud why the vast new expenditures on lavishly equipped open plan schools, on teacher training colleges, on sound and visual aids and recreational facilities, has failed to pay off in the shape of an informed and purposeful younger generation technically and morally equipped to take charge of their future.

But it has not identified the root causes of the crop failure. It has apparently failed to tackle the blight at its origin. The earnest but visually handicapped horticulturist, tearing his hair out because so many of his prize cabbages and lettuces are turning yellow under the rays of the noonday sun, focusses his tunnel vision on a remote corner of the nurseries, and fails to see that a staff assistant is casually watering the nearby seedlings with a solution of sodium chlorate or Jeyes' fluid. Is that it? Or are we confronted with the blindness of those who will not see?

¶ 63 THE PLOY THAT NORMAN TEBBIT FOILED

Proof that the humanists were still burrowing insidiously into the English educational system came in November of 1981 in a disclosure from Mr. Norman Tebbit, recently appointed Employment Secretary in the Thatcher Government. Parents from his own constituency had complained to him that their children were suffering psychological distress as a result of "multi-ethnic" experiments conducted at the local Rushcroft High School, whereby the elevens and twelves were formally persuaded in a series of classroom sessions that their intelligence was directly related to the proportions of their heads, and that those who had been misendowed with the wrong size of top piece must assume they were permanently disadvantaged.

Later in the curriculum, when the kids had well and truly acquired a complex about their inferior status, it would be explained to them that their distress and feelings of inferiority had been artificially induced so that they might better understand what it felt like to be part of a minority group, as for instance black people living in a predominantly white environment. One wonders whether, having once been made the victims of such a sick practical joke, the pupils at Rushcroft High School were ever going to believe their teachers again. But this notwithstanding, Mr. Tebbit was promptly branded as an enemy of "multi-cultural education" because he prevailed upon the local education authority to terminate the experiments. The luminary who allowed himself to be quoted in this context was a certain Harold Rosen, Professor of English at London University's Educational Institute, — from which we can gather that Professor Rosen is one of those trendy educators actively involved in the humanisation of our schools.

¶ 64 SENSITIVITY TRAINING

The sociological ploy which Norman Tebbit so righteously exposed at Rushcroft had already appeared in a variety of other guises in American schools. Barbara Morris, in her booklet entitled

"Why are You Losing Your Children?", describes the technique as "sensitivity training", — and categorises it as part of a process whereby a child is gradually made to shed all its parental teaching, its religious beliefs and its individualist leanings in favour of group or collective values. The open plan school and group discussion sessions have been deliberately introduced and popularised for this type of indoctrination.

The teacher, or "facilitator", picks on one pupil who might appear to have a personal or social problem, and asks him or her to explore and ventilate that problem in front of the class, who will be invited to assist with a solution. Hang-ups, repressions and fantasies, as well as doctrinal beliefs and child-parent differences, can often be brought out for the morbid inspection of classmates by this method, and according to Morris it often results in traumas which the "facilitator" or "educator" is totally unqualified to control. Also a young person's values are generally not clearly enough defined to enable him to defend them against hostile questioning, and it takes a strong personality to resist.

Once such an experiment has worked its way round a class or discussion group, with repetitive *critiques* of home, family religion and attitudes, all that remain are "group" values. The individual has been constrained into conforming with the group norms established under the discussion process, and it must be expected that many of those group or consensus values will have been skilfully inserted by the "educator". Once a child has been persuaded out of his or her traditional beliefs or family-inspired credos, this progress is regarded as a *"behavioural gain"*.

With some justification, Barbara Morris claims that this emphasis on *sensitivity training* is responsible for the generation-gap psychosis which has become a feature of American society during those last few decades, and certainly nothing would seem more deliberately orientated to exacerbate family differences as between the young and their elders. When one has been given an opportunity to examine what those new-style *educators* are up to, one need not be unduly surprised if youngsters subjected to this pernicious reversal of their childhood values should tend to distance themselves emotionally from parents whose disciplines and traditional beliefs their classroom discussions have discredited.

¶ 65 KILLING CHRISTIANITY WITH FAINT PRAISE

An aspect of sensitivity training which should not be missed, — especially in a volume which concerns itself with the survival of the Christian faith, — is its inbuilt capacity for attacking religion. In the humanist scheme of things all religions are equal, though they obviously have planned it in such a way that their own creed, humanism, will be more equal than all the others.

Humanist teachers do not object to taking religious instruction, but they believe that such instruction should not be orientated towards any particular faith, — should in fact be treated in a general way, illustrating the main features and doctrines of all the principal world religions without indicating preference for any. In other words, they would explain to their pupils what other people believe, whilst themselves preserving an attitude of urbane detachment which might be more impressive to questioning young minds than snatches of the Gospel sandwiched between slices of the Koran and the Hindu vedas.

In the United States the original reason for taking orthodox religion out of the schools was the proliferation of sects and ethnic minorities who objected to purely Christian teaching. Latterly this has also become a valid pretext in Britain, where, following years of surreptitious immigration from the coloured Commonwealth, morning prayers in many urban schools came to be attended by children of various colours and creeds who had either never heard of the white man's Messiah, or were thirled to the customs of the Near East and Asia.

So it seemed to be merely a concession to the obvious when in November of 1980 the headmaster of the Matthew Moss Middle School in Rochdale, Lancashire, announced that he was dropping the predominantly Christian bias from his morning assembly because twenty per cent of his intake were from Moslem or similar religious backgrounds. He proposed to replace it with a "comprehensive" assembly which would be acceptable to all religions, — or presumably also to those with no religion at all.

His announcement brought an outraged reaction from a single Rochdale clergyman, who reminded the headmaster that they were still living in a Christian country. "I don't believe in retreat," he said. "I believe in tolerance. We would like to show Christian tolerance towards others, but reserve the right to pursue our Christianity without making concessions."

¶ 66 BEHIND THE ULSTER KILLINGS

That Rochdale vicar was right of course. By its very nature Christianity is a tolerant faith, but it can be betrayed by those who go on making concessions. In these days of diminishing attendance at church and Sunday school, the morning prayers and periods of religious instruction may be the only occasions when many a child makes contact with those doctrines of mercy, forgiveness and eventual salvation which provide all that is best in the society into which he was born. All right for the little Hindu or Moslem, Jew or committed non-believer to absent himself from those sessions, as the 1944 Education Act allows! This is a privilege that has been exercised by the nonconforming down through the years, and it caused neither stress nor embarrassment until the humanists came along with their subtle orientation towards a pluralist society in which there would be no clearly defined doctrine of belief other than humanistic values.

Those who allow themselves to be influenced by considerations of ethnic and religious minorities, — as did that headmaster in Rochdale, — or by the persistent calls for desegregation of denominational schools in the United Kingdom, should be aware whose purposes they are unwittingly serving. The drive for the abolition of church schools, and indeed for the eventual removal of religious teaching from school curriculums, is powered and guided by the British Humanist Association, which is not beyond seizing upon the religious bigotry in Northern Ireland as an example of what can happen through sectarian rivalries within the same Christian faith.

There is at least an indication that all true Ulster Christians, from whatever side of the sectarian divide, have long ago recoiled in horror from the consequences of religious intolerance in that macabre situation, and if the British at large have been shocked at the brutal insensitivity of the killings, they should also be touched by the heroism of those who have dared to preach harmony and conciliation in the face of threats and draconian retribution. There is nothing of God or His mercy in any of the murderous strife which for a whole decade has scarred the social and business life of Ireland's northern counties. Neither is the I.R.A. a legitimate implement of the Roman Catholic faith. It has long ago been subverted and politicised, and moulded into an instrument of revolutionary terror linked to the Red Brigades of Europe and the Marxist Internationale.

¶ 67 THE ATTEMPT TO TAKE RELIGION OUT OF THE CLASSROOM

So let no one shake you out of your denominational convictions just because Christians are apparently practising internecine warfare on other Christians in Belfast or Crossmaglen. The humanists may not have created the Irish troubles, but they are intent on turning them to their own advantage, — and to them the ultimate advantage would be an end to segregation and the total abolition of religious observance or instruction from school curriculums.

All right! you may have some sympathy with the argument that segregated schools are socially divisive, that they do on occasions breed bigotry, intolerance and violence. You may feel so strongly about the perpetuation of such abuses that you are willing to support almost any reform that is aimed at their elimination. But think the matter through in the light of what the humanists intend for all our futures.

We are still a Christian people because we still have an established church in each of the member countries of the United Kingdom. That church is entitled to impress its moral codes and its doctrines upon all the practices and institutions of the state. *Especially is it both empowered and encouraged to carry its message into the schools at a time when young minds are at their most impressionable.*

The humanists propose to change all that. If they are allowed to have their way, Christianity will descend from its supreme place in our minds and hearts, and compete for our allegiance with secular philosophies such as Communism, Marxism, Maoism and humanism itself. They are, as always, fair-seeming and tolerant as they detail how the changes should be applied. They do not suggest that there should be any restriction upon Christian teaching in designated places of worship. Neither do they deny the right of parents to try and influence their children into following their own faith. They would not have us do away with Sunday schools, bible classes, choir practices or hymn-singing of an evening at the youth fellowship. But they insist that each child has a right to choose, — and they plan for him to choose in an environment where their own materialistic creed will have more than an even chance of taking root.

All great religious and philosophical movements have had their periods of militant evangelism. This is the age of the secular humanist, and such is his capacity for directing trends and innovating ideas behind the scenes that he is likely to complete his conquest without the madding world being aware of it, — that is, unless we can start to unravel some of his schemes in their early stages, and get ordinary folks to show an interest.

We should talk about humanism, you and I, — talk about it openly and persistently, — exposing its hypocrisies and its manipulations wherever these come to our notice. Let's not be inhibited by the fact that none of the foregoing material will ever be allowed to appear in the leader columns of our favourite newspaper. It's an undercover ploy if ever there was, and it's specially formulated to lull the sensibilities of nice polite people like you and you, — who would simply not be so presumptuous as to question the motives of a professor of education.

Friend! Fellow parent! Fellow Christian! don't be so *civilised* about it all. Find out what's going on with your kids in the classroom. And if you don't like it, get in there and make your opinions known.

CHAPTER VIII

¶ 68 THE PERVERSIONS OF J. M. KEYNES

So at this stage what is your most representative character amongst the bunch of humanitarian idealists who would lead us into a humanistic future? The trendy Scottish philosopher Boyd Orr, with his obsessions about a hungry world on an over-crowded planet? Walter Mondale, smooth-talking diplomat who became Jimmy Carter's vice-president in 1977? John D. Rockefeller III, millionaire Wall Street banker and leading exponent of World Population Control? The renowned English academic Julian Huxley, who dominated the early sessions of the United Nations Educational, Scientific and Cultural Organisation? Dr. Benjamin Spock, the professing child psychologist whose novel theories on discipline in the home turned many a normal child into a juvenile monster? Jawaharlal Nehru, first Prime Minister of an independent India? Dag Hammarskjold, U.N. Secretary-General who presided over so many of the World Body's dubious adventures in Africa? Or turning back to the nineteenth century and the origins of the cult, — George Bernard Shaw, the Irish dramatist of telling phrase and caustic wit who helped found the Fabian Society; Robert Morss Lovett, the American Fabian who hated his native land so intensely that he wanted to connive at its total destruction; Jean-Paul Sartre, French Marxist author and visionary of the new society?

All prominent people who exerted considerable influence upon their respective generations, — and all probably characterised as having *progressive* and even *permissive* ideas! Disciples of a new trend in social and religious acceptability! Maybe you had not previously realised that all those well-known people were humanists, but now that you see them associated, they do seem to have some things in common.

Any of them recognised as being kinky or abnormal? Well, Dag Hammarskjold, who as Secretary-General of the U.N. was one of the most influential men in the entire world, was also a lonely homosexual whose abnormality was said to have coloured many of the bizarre decisions taken during his period of office. And humanism as a creed, as a new *stance for living,* seems to have gathered under its banner so many of the sexually and socially maladjusted. Havelock Ellis, contemporary of Bernard Shaw and the Webbs, and author of the massive *Studies in the Psychology of Sex,* which would become a future text book for humanist sex educators, was himself a sexual deviant of a particularly repulsive kind. The Bloomsbury Socialist circle which orbited around the family and associates of Karl Marx, and which nurtured such future notables as Lytton Strachey and J. M. Keynes, practised every form of sexual abuse and aberration from free love, through bi-sexual masochism to lesbianism, sodomy and paedophilia.

John Maynard Keynes himself, known variously as the originator of interventionist capitalism, and as the father of socialist economics, was apparently another of those abnormal creatures who found no lasting satisfaction in the frills, frailties and seductive embraces of the other sex, preferring to found favoured and jealously protected relationships with other men. In common with his friend and sometime paramour Lytton Strachey, he is also reported to have made frequent visits to the Arabic cities of the Mediterranean, where in that particular era poor families were apparently willing to sell their male children into prostitution for the perverted pleasure of aberrant English aristocratic socialists.

It is said of Keynes that from his Cambridge days onwards he had the uncanny knack of seeking out corruptible human material from amongst his many relationships, and that he did in fact corrupt every susceptible being who came within his reach. He is best known for the economic theory which bears his name, but we in this volume will find more relevance in his lesser publicised pronouncements upon religion, and upon the Christian code of morals, which he found to be both offensive and distasteful, — perhaps because it recoiled in horror from the depravities of his own existence.

Even so it was the Keynesian code of sexual licence and permissiveness which was destined to be perpetuated in the humanist manifesto and in the policies of humanist educators, whilst the upholders of the Christian ethic would by contrast find themselves fighting a forlorn rearguard action. A confirmed atheist, debauchee and pervert like J. M. Keynes would naturally have no time for Christian marriage, or for the traditional and honourable role of women in a Christian society. A hopeless deviant himself, he seems to have had the brilliance and persuasiveness to induce perversions in others, and with Oscar Wilde he was a forerunner of that homosexual old boys' network which flourished in England's top drawer universities, and which in the immediate pre-war generation would throw up perverted traitors like Guy Burgess, Donald MacLean and the former M.I.5 chief Kim Philby.

Keynes' attitude to the existing law in its treatment of sexual offences and abnormalities might also have been the inspiration behind the Wolfenden and Kinsey Reports, which advocated, and did eventually establish, the legitimacy of homosexual relations between consenting adults, — a development subsequently followed by a demand for 'gay' rights and privileges even to the extent of marriage between two people of the same sex.

¶ 69 "NEITHER MARRY NOR ARE GIVEN IN MARRIAGE"

These illuminating references to the depraved sex life and aberrant tendencies of a famous father figure of modern humanism should come readily to mind when we consider how the deviant tendencies of our abnormally endowed fellow citizens have come to exert quite an unbalanced influence upon our modern society. Since the vindication of Wolfenden and Kinsey, homosexuals have moved into dominating positions in the artistic world, into drama, news gathering and the business of mass communication. There has for some time been a strong suspicion of a virtual takeover in some of our television studios, where in such cloistered atmospheres the abnormal can become the normal, and the heterosexual a curiosity from the platitudinous world outside.

Nevertheless, despite snide remarks and possible indications to the contrary, it is no intention of this volume to 'knock' the sexually aberrant. The author does not accept that homosexuality is a vice born entirely out of frustration in the dormitories of English public schools. Neither does he believe that it can be ignored, suppressed as an unclean thing by the puritanical vetos of earlier centuries. There is evidence that it can be artificially and unhealthily stimulated, that it will flourish unnaturally as a cult and a fashion trend in too congenial surroundings, that it will on occasions deprave its practitioners and corrupt their victims.

But when the *kooks* and the *kinks* have been eliminated, when we have absorbed the scandalous sensationalism of men stripping down for the gratification of other men, and women defying biology to snuggle up to other women, there remains a basic problem for a minority of our fellow beings, that the instincts with which they were born cause them to shrink from trans-sexual relationships. Some, neutral in their desires, ask only to be left in peace. Others, imbued with strong if abnormal impulses, and unwilling to contemplate the life of loneliness to which heterosexual society would condemn them, employ a variety of fetishes and a series of age-old flag signals to seek out those kindred spirits with similar emotional propensities to their own.

Let's all show a bit more broadmindedness and understanding about these matters than we have tended to do in the past. Let's also exhibit, as from within the Holy Christian Church, that charity and goodfellowship which the Redeemer truly intended to encompass all men and all women, of whatever shades, manners and predilections. One may from time to time encounter a deep-set impression that those who exhibit homosexual tendencies cannot be Christians because their inborn impulses run counter to the established habits of the heterosexual majority. Modern medicine and psychiatry can occasionally be contradictory on the subject, their diagnosis ranging from the genetic to the psychological. But whether or not the condition is responsive to treatment, — whether or not the average aberrant individual is anxious for treatment, — it is a condition which exists in fact, and need not be an obstacle to faith.

There is in Christ's teaching at least one reference which should induce us to proceed with caution, if not compassion. As reported from St. Matthew's Gospel, at Chapter 22 and verse 30, He tells us that "in the resurrection they neither marry nor are given in marriage, but are as the angels of God in Heaven".

What are we to take from this illuminating sentence? That sex and gender, — and genes and odd abnormal impulses, — are attributes of our earthly bodies which do not become perpetuated in the immortal soul? It would be a pity if we could not probe more deeply into the eternal truths on that one, for the fact of the matter is that homosexuals, many of them talented and artistic people, have been drawn in considerable numbers to the hedonistic cult of humanism, — not because they share its materialistic doctrine, but because thus far the Christian community has not found an acceptable way of accommodating them within the fold.

¶ 70 PORNOGRAPHY, AND VIOLENCE AGAINST WOMEN

It is, however, important to ensure that none of the sympathy which we reserve for the genetically confused can be read as a prompter to perversion. We live in an age when the *kooks* and the *kinks* are rampant, — and when Gay Rights groups are openly aggressive and demanding. Homosexual and lesbian relationships are featured to such effect on television dramas that one might almost expect them to become the norm. Sex shops are opening on many a local high street, ready to provide the fetichist and the pervert with everything from prefabricted chest hair to imitation male and female genitalia. And then there's the porn!

So what is porn? Porn, you might say, is sex with a suggestive leer. It is a shamefaced indulgence in lewd and unnatural desires which a man would hesitate to try upon his wife, and would certainly not communicate to his daughters. It is cheap access to a fantasy world of the libertine and the sadist. It is a pandering to the basest instincts in human nature, — and it pays well, which shows that it seldom lacks for customers. A lot of people with money to spend are apparently hooked on porn. Its perniciousness and its commercial success are linked with our attitudes to sex itself.

And sex, of course, with its tendernesses, its impulses, its wonderful heartwarming splendours, is the great throbbing emotion which makes the world go round. It channels and epitomises most of the love, sweetness, sacrifice and heroics of which humanity is capable. If men were ever civilised, rationalised or chemically neutered so as to be unmoved at sight of a trim hemline or a shapely leg, — if women ever stopped having the instinct for physical love with lusty he-men, — then we would be well on the way to test-tube biology and a race of neurotic humanoids. Sex and its satisfaction in wholesome, highly intimate personal relationships, is the greatest and most lasting of life's joys. What a shame that such a wonderful thing can so often be degraded!

In December of 1980 a group of angry women were demonstrating in the Midlands city of Coventry. They called themselves *Women against Violence against Women,* and their protest had come at the end of a horrifying series of sex murders by a sadistic killer known as the Yorkshire Ripper. They were complaining about the prostitution and degradation of the female body through the persistence of pornography, and about the level of sexual violence that had become too readily acceptable in a society which continually paid lip service to women's rights and liberties. The cinema, having lost its mass market to television, was endeavouring to win back customers by crude sensationalism, and it had been deemed a box office attraction to depict women in defenceless poses, where they were easily ravished and murdered. Despite the compassionate and caring society, men's attitudes remained cynical and unsympathetic, recorded incidences of rape had been rising steadily for a whole decade, and there was a general climate of fear.

¶ 71 TRACKING DOWN THE PROMOTERS

What had caused it? Why was it less safe for a woman to walk down a darkened street than it had been ten, fifteen or twenty years previously? The dirty magazines? The pin-ups? The pornographic

"Drama-play enactments of human debauchery have a sedating effect on the sexually unbalanced."

Humanist psychiatrist

films? The larger than life exposures of alluring feminine attributes in technicolour on a thousand-and-one hoardings up and down the country? The depiction on king-size cinerama screens of lust, sadism and kinky violence?

Humanistic psychiatrists would insist that such drama-play enactments of human debauchery had actually a sedating effect upon the sexually unbalanced, who might then be less inclined to act out their fantasies in real life. But tell that to the distraught woman who, prudent if revolted, has just stripped to the navel in a lonely alley so that she could be sex-objectisised at knife point by some teenage punk fresh from the latest sadistic smash-hit at the local bughouse.

It was reported, rather quaintly, that those W.A.V.A.W. demonstrators, many of them female liberationists and women's rights activists, had been somewhat confused and disconcerted to find themselves belatedly and uncharacteristically on the same side as the redoubtable Mary Whitehouse, whose one-woman campaign to ban pornographic sex, sadism and violence from cinema, radio and television, had at one time exposed her to lampooning, satire and sniggering ridicule at the hands of the entire liberal establishment. Suddenly the women's libbers were beginning to notice that in two decades of social revolution women had somehow become publicly degraded,—and their instinctive reaction was to blame it on men.

But what men? The men who made the films, ran the sex shops, wrote and distributed the pornographic literature? The men who liberalised the censorship laws and made it all perfectly legal? The financiers who promoted it from behind the scenes and allegedly made vast fortunes out of female humiliation and environmental insecurity? The humanists? Anyone willing to try a long shot, and have a stab at blaming the humanistic revolution for the upsurge in sexual violence?

¶ 72 ABORTION AND STERILISATION

At first sight it might seem unlikely. With their obsession about people control and curbing population growth, a logical extension of the humanist philosophy would be towards some moderation of the sex drive, — a toning down of human promiscuity. Perhaps, with their leanings towards the drug industry, the advocacy of some otherwise harmless serum which would dampen down the ardours of eroticism, and reduce desire to a socially acceptable norm! All this along with a carefully orchestrated campaign towards restraint and self denial in heterosexual contact! Continence! Chastity! Sublimation of the entire reproductive impulse in an overcrowded world where we might eventually be threatened with babies on the ration card!

Is that how you think the humanists might, — or ought — to have played it? And having by now had some conception of their vast powers of influence and persuasion as they bring their ideas into practice, have you seen any signs in recent years that such a campaign of restraint and sexual modesty is quietly developing?

No? Well you don't surprise me. For in point of fact the humanists seem to have approached the problem from the opposite direction. Through the U.N.'s Planned Parenthood Federation they had made a start by promoting legalised abortion in all those Western countries where the opposition of the Roman Catholic Church was not strong enough to prevent it. The success of that manoeuvre in reducing unwanted births may have indicated that there were other ways of achieving population control than by the discouragement of heterosexual intimacies.

What about proliferating sexuality in all its excesses, promiscuities, perversities and aberrations, to such an extent that it would be stripped of all its wonderful allure and mystery, becoming instead a kind of commercialised peepshow that would stimulate the kinks, the kooks and the deviants? Where it also resulted in an increase of normal trans-sexual activity, this could easily be contained by the vast refinements in sterility and contraception which medical science was then bringing into practical application. And is this not a close approximation to what has actually been happening?

¶ 73 SHELTERING THE PAEDOPHILIAC

We know positively that population control is one of the principal aims of humanism. Sir Julian Huxley, the celebrated British humanist who became first Director-General of U.N.E.S.C.O., indicated in his official writings that he regarded control of human breeding as an ultimate object of his organisation,—and the multi-millionaire John D. Rockefeller III, whose family foundation had contributed to many humanist causes, chaired President Johnson's Committee on Population and Family Planning, besides publishing a book in which he expressed an opinion that *his* might be the last generation for which the begetting of children could be a voluntary choice.

So once you had got over the moral and technical problems of interfering with human biology, a surfeit of sex, — callous, enforced or sadistic, — was no hindrance to the population planners since it need not reach the birth statistics. Also, where sex stimulants emphasised and sensationalised the abnormal, in so far as they increased the incidence of buggery and sodomy they siphoned off some of the excess desire which might otherwise have been channelled into reproduction.

It has already been pointed out that the humanists appear to have gotten themselves a corner in the market for perversion. One is unable to say whether all way-out perverts are humanists, — and it would certainly be unwise, and indeed inaccurate, to argue that all humanists are perverts. But a philosophy which looked back in retrospect to such a father figure as John Maynard Keynes could not refrain from an endeavour to give sex deviancies and abnormalities an aura of respectability.

In March of 1981, in a row which involved the invoking of parliamentary privilege, a Tory M.P., Geoffrey Dickenson, insisted upon the public exposure of a retired high-ranking diplomat who had been associated with a pervert organisation called the Paedophile Information Exchange, whose speciality was the circulation of pornographic material about the esoteric pleasures of sex with young children. Dickenson incurred the considerable wrath of the Establishment by this exposure. It was pointed out, somewhat testily, by the Attorney General that the diplomat had been retired for some years before his aberrant tendencies came to light, and that there was no legal relevance in pressing the matter, since his only implication had been in the trafficking of obscene literature through the public mail, — not a penal offence where it has not been done for commercial gain.

But of course you and I realise that there was a vital public interest to be served outwith the cloistered atmosphere of the House of Commons. Sir Peter Hayman, the diplomat in question, had been identified as a paedophile, and as such, he and colleagues of like mind within the civil service establishment might naturally be expected to deal sympathetically with similar aberrations where it came within their jurisdiction.

Yet paedophilia is not a perversion which invites any degree of sympathy or understanding from the public at large. It is an abuse and a monstrosity which may continue to lurk perversely in the secret minds of outwardly respectable citizens, but which for the good of society should never be allowed to see the light of day. In the early years of the twentieth century Keynes and his paramour Lytton Strachey might have been able to indulge their deviant impulses in a milieu where it was not socially unacceptable. The impoverished Moorish families of that day, we are told, were resigned to juvenile prostitution as a means of supplementing their meagre incomes, and had conditioned themselves to paedophilia as a sort of tourist industry.

But the same bestial and unnatural instincts, where they are nurtured and sheltered by deviants within our own establishment, and where they are free to snatch the occasional unwary victim from our highways and byways, need not and cannot be allowed the same tolerant compliance. For those of limited scholarship in Greek derivatives, and a corresponding lack of response to euphemistic innuendos, it may now be time to put things a bit more crudely, — to call a spade a spade, and a paedophiliac a potential sex murderer of a particularly harrowing and revolting type.

Those parents whose children are inclined to wander, and who become justifiably uptight and nervous when the youngsters fail to come home at the appointed hour, may think instinctively of all the unattended pitshafts, quarries and stretches of stagnant water in their own immediate vicinity. Police and volunteers who from time to time find themselves involved in one of those heartbreaking searches for a missing child, dredge canals, ransack the attics and crumbling fabric of empty disused houses and factories, open every door, scour every ditch and runnel, overturn every makeshift shack and hovel where an adventurous boy might have got himself entrapped. But from recent experience they know in their minds and hearts that accident and natural calamity cover only half of the possibilities which they might eventually have to take back to bereaved and sorrowing parents.

Children who wander alone in the darkness of our decaying towns and cities, or in the woodlands stretches of our quiet countryside, occasionally fall victim to a predator whose antisocial impulses may go for ever undetected because they go side by side with an outward respectability which puts the possessor above suspicion in his own community. No one with normal instincts can imagine what transpires in those gruesome moments when a terrified juvenile succumbs to the unnatural lust of a perverted adult. What we do know is that the encounter is so often fatal for the object of that perverted passion, which discards the immature little body when it has done with it.

¶ 74 KILLING FOR KICKS — NO EFFECTIVE RETRIBUTION

So those Women Against Violence Against Women have something else to worry them as a result of the permissive revolution which they had originally hailed with such glee. Not only do they have to be wary of sex-crazed lunatics who want to strip them of their decency in a darkened car park, but if they have youngsters at home, they have also to ward against the nightmare that some local nutcase, stimulated by the porn put out by a paedophiliac information bureau, might pick on one of their own little ones to satisfy his abnormal craving.

It would partly have come about due to that progressive slackening of the penal code, particularly in respect of murder and insensate violence, which meant that there was no longer any credible deterrent against killing for the sake of killing, or for sexual kicks and way-out esoteric experiences; partly due to the "enlightened" climate in which sex deviancies were analysed and publicised and given the accolade of social acceptability. Anyone still have serious doubts that the humanists played a significant part in these developments? Any stubborn liberal apologist ready to draw his sword on their behalf, to cry insult and infamy upon such as would accuse those urbane, high-minded sophisticates of conduct likely to contribute to the breakdown of social order? If so, let him keep his weapon at the ready. For we're still coming at him. With the spirit of John Maynard Keynes still a haunting memory, we're now going to examine the humanist record on sex education.

CHAPTER IX

¶ 75 STIMULATING AN INTEREST IN SEX

The 1960's saw a veritable deluge of books and pamphlets on sexual matters, all purporting to be dissatisfied with the degree of public interest that was shown in sex, with the manner in which young people learned about sex, with the amount of information that was readily available about sex and sexual problems. You and I, who lived through those 1960's, were probably not aware of any sudden crises arising in our heterosexual lives or in the society of those around us. Boys were meeting girls, kissing in shady nooks and indulging in emotional experiences which might — or might not — end up in permanent relationships or marriage. Fathers and mothers, with the benefits of hindsight to guide them, were basically following the same emotional pattern, sometimes with their own partners, sometimes with other people's. It was essentially a discreet and intimate business. Men might not have been growing more virile and more handsome, but aided by good health, modern hygiene and a fashion industry that surely knew how to present its wares, women were undoubtedly growing more attractive, more exasperatingly alluring. It was a good age in which to be young and lusty, and possessed of a normal sexual appetite. Was there any substantial minority that felt *deprived* of fundamental knowledge?

Mostly we thought not. But even so there were certain high-sounding and pretentious organisations getting very concerned. These had their origins, — and their power base, — in the United

Nations, which in the thirty-five years of its existence has already been responsible for some very odd decision and policy making.

In this case they had decided there *was* a crisis, whether *we* were aware of it or not. Sexual ignorance was acting as a drag and an obstruction upon the building of the new world order. Children in particular were being deprived of information that was essential to their fuller participation in a more enlightened future. In modern day conditions there was no guarantee that the necessary instruction would be available in the home, — yet the teaching was urgently needed *because of the way in which sex was being emphasised and commercialised through the mass media . . .*

Yes, stop there and wait for it. We are once again in the syndrome of *the old one-two.* For who have we just discovered to be the main promoters of commercialised sex, — and who can command enough power and influence to make an impression on the mass communications industry whenever they are so minded? No prizes for the answer! You've met those humanists before. Now you're going to meet them again, — and on familiar ground. First they work like beavers to create the problem, then they extol its frightening social consequences, — finally they propose their solution.

The solution in this case was to be a worldwide programme of sex education that would take the secrets of the bedroom into Primary Six, or even lower. Little Johnny and his sister Mary, their big eyes opened wonderingly, were going to learn in the classroom all the lush and leery curiosities of the reproductive cycle.

As we know from previous samplings of the humanist plan for education, it was not going to stop at a factual demonstration of the purely animal functions which ensure the continuity of the human race. Along with this early exposure to the physical side of sex, children would also be subjected to that muddying of their ethical and moral values which comes with "situation ethics". They would be taught, in confoundation of the scriptures, that human beings are essentially creatures of their environment, and cannot be held individually responsible for their actions.

Easy to see, isn't it, how after a few years of this hedonistic philosophy, the primary schools of America's multiracial inner cities had degenerated into blackboard jungles, with security guards patrolling the corridors to keep the resulting violence, sadism and vandalism from escalating out of control? Easy to see also why juvenile courts and probation services in both Britain and America were finally unable to cope with the demands made upon them, as they were overwhelmed by a whole generation of young anarchists lacking scruples or moral values, who just *knew* that their objectionable manners and criminal attitudes were not their responsibility, but the fault of the System, — who had also been quick to realise the helplessness and inadequacies of the police, law courts and penal establishments in face of their total renunciation of society's codes of legitimate behaviour.

¶ 76 THE FABIAN-HUMANIST-MARXIST OCTOPUS

So they had done it again, hadn't they, those progressive thinkers with the advanced ideas, who in a spirit of altruistic concern were preparing us for the twenty-first century? First they had invented *situation ethics* so that kids could be rid of their guilt complexes when they went on the rampage. Then they created departments of child psychiatry to analyse the origins and causes of juvenile delinquency. Latterly they would come up with a solution . . .

Hard to swallow it all down in one big indigestible lump, isn't it,—this concept that an assorted bunch of academic agnostics, atheistic philosophers, religious humanists, United Nations directors, Population Control enthusiasts, Wall Street millionaire bankers and Marxist revolutionaries should first of all *want* to make such an awful mess of moral codes which had served us well through nearly two thousand years of Christendom; and *secondly,* should jointly possess the resources, ingenuity, deviousness and downright dedication to make so many of their policies come true?

Impressions of a band of anarchical conspirators meeting by candlelight in some rat-infested basement are of course illusory and wholly inaccurate. Yet it must be difficult for the ordinary citizen to accept that a creed and a philosophy spearheaded by a few scholarly academics could in a few short years change the behavioural patterns of an entire generation. What has to be remembered in this context is that humanism is but one of a group of co-related moral, political and economic philosophies, comprising Fabianism, Keynesianism, Marxism and Communism, all of which have a common ideological bond, — and all of which, when they pull together collectively, are capable of exerting enormous influence. Many of those who have struggled against it must often have felt that they were squirming in the tentacles of an octopus, such is its capacity to protect its own, and to obstruct and hinder the unwelcome intruder. You and I are now classed as intruders.

¶ 77 DR. MARY CALDERONE OF S.I.E.C.U.S.

In the matter of sex education, the humanists scarcely bothered to conceal their strategic inspiration or their tactical involvement. The Sex Information and Educational Council of the United States, which was founded round about 1965, got its early guidance and promptings from the humanists at U.N.E.S.C.O., and according to the painstaking researches of Claire Chambers in *The SIECUS Circle,* all of its six departmental directors had impeccable humanist credentials of their own.

So why this pressure for sex education in the later decades of the twentieth century? And why did it have to be a purely humanist organisation which planned its introduction? Back to that bit about *commercialised sex,* and the manner in which it was being exploited through the mass media! When pressed, the founders of S.I.E.C.U.S. would argue disarmingly that they had been *invited* into existence because of the increasing amount of pornographic material that was being made available to the young, who would surely get a healthier and more balanced version of the facts of life from classroom studies than from the peep show or the burlesque.

Point taken! But Chambers reports rather significantly that Dr. Mary Calderone, the visionary and guiding genius of S.I.E.C. in the United States, the lady who has been given unstinting praise for bringing so many of its plans to fruition, was herself married to a theatre-owner who was not beyond staging sex shows as a form of public entertainment. In fact, during the years when the crusading Dr. Calderone was labouring to make S.I.E.C.U.S. a predominant guiding force within the American primary schools system, her husband Frank was having trouble with the censors in a Long Island district where one of his theatres was situated. They described the highlight of his burlesque show there as being both lewd and obscene.

All right! women cannot always be held responsible for the morals of the men they marry. So perhaps the visionary Dr. Mary was putting her heart and soul into the promotion of S.I.E.C.U.S. as a counterblast to the sex-saturation and sex symbolism in which her own husband was commercially involved. In that case we would expect to have from her some uplifting public pronouncement reassuring to the parents of those many thousands of American children who would get their initiation into sex and sexuality by means of Calderone methodology.

No such reassurance is currently available. Mary S. Calderone received the 1974 award as Humanist of the Year from the American Humanist Association, and her anti-religious views have on more than one occasion been broadcast through the media and the Tv networks. She is known to favour the merging or reversing of the sex roles in social life, the alienation of children from their parents, and the eventual abolition of the family unit, — all highly contentious viewpoints which, through the subtleties of *sensitivity training* and *situation ethics,* would give a sex-deviationist and pronounced anti-Christian slant to S.I.E.C. syllabuses as they filtered down to the classroom.

Dr. Calderone's associations and sympathies with other campaigning groups and personalities are also relevant in this context. She was listed as medical director of the Rockefeller-promoted Planned Parenthood-World Population Control for a number of years previous to formation of the Sex Information and Educational Council, and when considering the education of her own daughter, opted for a socialist school in New York City founded by John Dewey and a group of other Fabian, humanist, Marxist and Communist International types devoted to the de-Christianisation and collectivisation of the United States.

¶ 78 SEX BIOLOGY FOR THE INFANTS

Atrocious, isn't it? Nigh unbelievable in fact! Through Rockefeller Foundation millionaire funding, through the sedulous activities of highly placed Fabians and humanists in health and educational

Sex biology in the Primary

departments of the U.S. Government, the master strategy for the twenty-first century in American primary school education was being entrusted to a self-confessed atheist and Fabian-humanist revolutionary with a pronounced bias against family life and orthodox Christian morality. This in a land which its thrusting and supremely self-confident citizens were once proud to hail as God's very own country!

Feeling smug, you denizens of those British islands, as you contemplate from afar the eventual eclipse and demoralisation of your transatlantic cousinry? Do not be so hasty. For, as has been previously noted in this series of volumes, so many of the ideas and innovations which originate on that side of the Atlantic soon find their way over here.

So it was to prove with the sexist educational methods of Dr. Mary Calderone and her fellow humanist luminaries in S.I.E.C.U.S. Material is already available, in presentable form, for carrying the Calderone message right into the British classroom, and due to the responsibility which is placed upon the ordinary headmaster for the selection of text books at his own particular school, it is at this level that the system can be penetrated.

Currently being promoted and circulated amongst educationists in the United Kingdom is a proposed teachers' guide to the early years of schooling which bears the title *All About Me.* Under the heading of "How Did I Begin?", this fair-seeming infant primer carries a full section on the reproductive cycle, including illustrated diagrams of animal and human foetuses within the womb, and a suggested question-and-answer session upon how a child is born. As to how babies are made, the manual describes how the man "places his penis into the vagina of the woman and after a while the seed passes through his penis into the woman where it might find its way to the egg".

All absolutely true of course! All well-proven and utterly irrefutable biological fact! But as classroom instruction for the under-eights? And as an intrusion upon their struggling efforts to master the abc's and the rudiments of English grammar? There are many well-meaning and unexceptionable sections of *All About Me,* such as its chapters upon nutrition, health and safety, — and these have no doubt been useful to the promoters in recommending it to the occasional trendy headmaster. But its heavy emphasis on play, food, health, social and extra-curricular activities as well as rudimentary sex biology, — all to the detriment of class discipline and formal instruction, — would ensure that our state comprehensives were never able to deliver up that level of academic and technical excellence which is required to meet the challenge of the future.

Christian education places its main emphasis upon development of the mind. It would seem that humanist educators are inordinately obsessed with the functions of the body. So which are we to choose,—Christian or humanist? In spite of soothing indications to the contrary, we cannot have both, since most of what we are revealing here shows that their aims are irreconcilable and contradictory.

¶ 79 O-LEVELS IN SEX DEVIANCIES AND BUGGERY

You didn't know half of what was going on,did you, — you hard-working ordinary citizen, — as you struggled to bring up a family in this modern age, and found that so many of the old values, which had been good enough for you and your father before you, were steadily and surreptitiously eroded, till you scarcely knew where to draw the line between right and wrong, between what was reasonable and progressive and what was fuddy-duddy and old-fashioned? You felt perhaps that it was a trend, something belonging to the era of the nuclear bomb, of jet travel, colour television, punk rock, women's lib., metrication and the Race Discrimination Act. You regretted it for what it was doing to your kids, but you thought that it was inevitable, — that it was futile to stand in the way of progress.

Well now perhaps you know different. Now perhaps you'll feel sufficiently involved to do something about it if your teenage daughter comes home and announces that she's doing a compulsory O-level course on sexual deviancies and buggery, as happened to some Yorkshire parents at the beginning of 1979. We use emotive language, of course, in order to get the point across. The course, set at Mirfield High School in West Yorks., was entitled Integrated Humanities, and seemed to cover everything from poverty and the family to sex with animals. As reported by the London *Daily Telegraph* of 29th January, the study material set by the Joint Matriculation Board on a previous occasion had contained obscenities laced with four-letter words.

And as a point of interest, those self-same four-letter words had always tripped readily enough from the lips of Dr. Mary Calderone, first executive director of S.I.E.C. in America, and mother and potential grandmother to sex education throughout the English-speaking world. So the munificent Rockefeller funding had already carried the ideological convictions and sexist obsessions of S.I.E.C.U.S. into respectable West Yorkshire homes. Shades of John Maynard Keynes, whose own depravities had made him scorn all that was normal and decent and cosily familial!

There are many fine, dedicated and thoroughly dependable teachers and administrators within our educational system. But as a result of the humanist pressures coming out through the United Nations, and the activities of such organisations as S.I.E.C.U.S. and its counterparts in the United Kingdom, there is also a smattering of creeps and perverts who grow bold as their ploys and practices are condoned in high places, — and who have to be carefully watched.

Especially do they have to be watched by an informed parent body which knows who they are, what motivates them, — and when they're up to no good. You, my friend, in your own little sphere, can do quite a bit to thwart the humanist revolution. Otherwise you also will be losing your children.

CHAPTER X

¶ 80 DRUG-SMUGGLING, VIOLENCE AND CRIME

Ever wondered who or what is behind the drug scene? All that stuff about tongs and triads, — and the theory that the devilish traffic in narcotics is a Chinaman's revenge on the Western World for its part in the nineteenth century opium trade! Or do you subscribe to the theory that it's all about money, — the immoral profits which are there to be made out of the trade in human bodies, out of the cravings of desperate addicts, who must be satisfied at whatever the sacrifice?

Money is a powerful incentive. Money can buy prestige and authority and seeming respectability, as well as corrupt or improvident policemen. Money can buy sealed lips. So also can the gun and the bomb, and the threat of maiming or disfigurement.

Drug smuggling and trafficking is big crime. Sometimes violent crime! It is also responsible for much of the incidental and irrational violence and law-breaking which has become a mind-boggling statistic of post-war police work, — and which has regrettably nullified so many of the enlightened social reforms aimed at creating a more just and equitable society.

No one bothers seriously to dispute this. The whole drug syndrome is universally abominated, and if there is one type of criminal who can be regarded as an utter social outcast, it is the drug-ring promoter, the smuggler and the pusher. Accordingly, no journalist or screen or television producer would dare to adopt a public viewpoint in which drug-taking or drug-running was portrayed as socially desirable.

That does not prevent the subject from making good box office. The activities of the narcotics branches of the various regional and national police forces have an irresistible appeal for the Tv viewer and the cinema-goer as they are seen to pit their wits against the shadowy monsters who peddle in human misery. In fact as well as in fiction, it can seem to be a nightmare world of intrigue and conspiracy, where evil is the norm rather than the exception. Reputably it is an entire underworld which makes its own laws and operates by its own code of practice. Retribution for the transgressor is generally swift and macabre, — and conducted on the old maxim that dead men tell no tales.

¶ 81 THE TRAFFIC WHICH NEVER ENDS

Are we satisfied with our conclusion that it is all about money, — money and the licentious profits which can be made by the really big operators in this atrocious trade? Do we accept that in the end it is just a commercial enterprise, — a filthy, illegal, immoral enterprise which flourishes perhaps both within and outwith the law, — which tots up its costs and its losses, and eventually pays fat dividends to some fantasised Mr. Big, who shall remain for ever in the shadows?

In drama and in fiction, where the anti-narcotics brigade has to achieve notable successes so as to accommodate the viewer's and the reader's sense of propriety, there is seldom an attempt, on the part of author or producer, to convey the feeling of total victory. Inevitably the agent with the name part and the star billing looks upon his triumph as a temporary advantage, as an episode to be repeated next week, when the beastly traffickers in human flesh have regrouped themselves and devised another ingenious scheme to flood the market with their illicit stock-in-trade.

In real life narcotics squads also have their successes. *Pushers* get caught, and are sent away for long terms of imprisonment. Agents and carriers are progressively exposed and eliminated, multi-million dollar consignments of addictive drugs are just occasionally detected, tracked down and taken into police hands. Entire drug rings are broken up, and their manufacturing and distributive networks destroyed. Yet even the brightest and most ambitious young anti-narcotics agent would never presume to imagine that he was working himself out of a job. Whatever the miracles of detection and observation achieved by himself and his small army of dedicated colleagues, this was a traffic which would just keep on coming.

¶ 82 ARE THERE CARTELS BEYOND THE LAW?

So what's behind it? Money? Money only? Or is there an ideological something or other which defies description and exposure? Amongst the front-line troops, the anti-drug squads of Scotland Yard and the F.B.I., there must be the occasional suspicion that they are up against something more complex than an illicit commercial empire, no matter how widespread and powerful. The tongs and the mafias have their acquired mystique, — they convey the impression of quasi-tribal groupings bound together by ethnic ties, and with a natural bent towards secrecy and conspiracy which might lead them into an underground war with Western society, especially if the profits could be funnelled back home to revive the glories of the ancestral village or fructify the family vineyards. The theory could be sustained if the vast majority of drug traffickers had a whiff of garlic on their breath, or lapsed into Cantonese under pressure of police questioning.

In reality of course the dupes, pushers, carriers, agents and tictac men who sustain the narcotics traffic are entirely international. They range from fallen members of the English aristocracy to deprived vagrants or coloured minorities in the back streets of Soho and Manhattan. Not all of them do it for gain. Many are themselves addicted, and are willing to accept their pay-offs as pushers and couriers partially in kind, all as a relatively cheap method of financing their own cravings.

Anti-narcotics men regard those pathetic specimens more as victims than exploiters of the trade in human degradation. They mop them up with the regularity of a cloakroom attendant mopping up a flooded washroom floor, but their ultimate concern, as always, is to try and locate the dripping tap.

Drug squads enjoy a favoured status in the law-enforcement hierarchy. They command impressive powers of search and in-depth investigation. But even they must from time to time be disturbingly aware that there are areas where they may not go, doors which, though they may knock, will not be opened. Privilege? The hint or suspicion that there are drug-smuggling cartels large and influential enough to obstruct the authorities in pursuit of their legitimate enquiries?

Or putting it another way, is there somewhere within our Western fabric of society a body of discreet but highly influential opinion which does not see drugs and drug-taking in the same detestable light as the rest of us, — an elite or an upper-crust whose teachings and whose attitudes lend an aura of respectability to the cult of smoking pot, rolling a reefer or getting high on LSD?

¶ 83 POP STARS AND DRUG ADDICTION

Where do the drug-pushers find an expanding market these days? On university campuses, where the college drop-outs, many from wealthy families, take to the addict's life of *highs* and hallucinations in preference to the grind of continued study? At high school parties, where the kids, pepped up with excitement and their first taste of alcohol, will run the risk of getting hooked on something more sinister when a more experienced companion promises them an exotic trip into a world of beautiful people and unimaginable fantasy? At pop concerts and way-out week-end music festivals held in open parkland, where the modern-day troubadours arrive with their guitars and bedrolls, transistors and hippie girl friends, — all geared up for forty-eight hours of mind-crazing, earsplitting cacophony?

Since the appearance of the Beatles in the nineteen-sixties, the pop scene and the drug scene were broadly complementary. All of the Beatles had taken drugs at one time or another, and due to the tremendous adulation which they enjoyed at the height of their fame, it was inevitable that thousands of their starry-eyed devotees should strive to emulate them in this, as well as in their other cults and eccentricities. Thus by their example they provided an unwitting boost to the narcotics industry, and it is remarkable how those otherwise unassuming young men, who made themselves considerable individual fortunes in their heyday, and created an entirely new tradition in the world of pop music, should have been almost continuously guided by nihilistic attitudes which bestowed a negative and essentially destructive influence upon the generation which jived and gyrated to their exciting new sound.

Even after they had split up, separate members of the Beatles quartet continued to indulge in the illicit weed, despite the hazards it must have presented to their freedom of action and professional reputations. Paul McCartney found himself shuttled home ignominiously at the beginning of a projected tour of Japan, because he had been caught with drugs in his possession. John Lennon, the guru of them all, became a legend as both a pornographer and a drug-taker; when he was finally shot down like a dog in a Manhattan street by one of his erstwhile fanatical admirers, 40,000 fans came to weep and mourn at his funeral, many of them doubtless ready customers for the pushers and street traders whom his own highly publicised addiction had helped to flourish.

Remember also the case of that English punk rock star who went under the repelling name of Sid Vicious, and who was arrested towards the end of 1978 by the New York police for the alleged murder of a former go-go dancer who was acting as his manager at the time? Vicious was addicted to hard drugs, a fact which would have considerable bearing on the case against him. Previous to the hearing, friends and professional contacts managed to secure his release on bail, and a party was held to celebrate the restoration of his personal freedom. Next morning he was found dead from an overdose of heroin. Police said he had been kept off the drug during his spell in jail, and his system was no longer able to cope with it. At the time of his death he was only twenty-one.

¶ 84 SEARCHING FOR NEW GODS TO WORSHIP

So by the late 'sixties there was in Britain and America, as well as in progressive countries of Continental Europe, at least one clearly indentifiable class or group of people who did not share the general public's utter detestation of the drug syndrome. The pop stars who followed the Beatles lived no less hectic lives, and finding themselves in an artificial world of hysteria and adulation, turned to cannabis, or sometimes something stronger, as a means of settling their nerves and seeking relaxation. The groupies caught on, as did a set of footloose youngsters, many of them from wealthy homes, who were anxious to be seen doing the "in" things, — and at that time the "in" thing was experimentation with drugs. Add to this the hippies and the drop-outs, the beautiful people and the flower people, the way-out sects, the zanies and the chronic sitdown protesters,— all that left-inclined, vaguely revolutionary mass of humanity who joined the propagandized peace rallies and the Vietnam war demonstrations. Not all of them were well enough heeled to pay for the extortionate cost of *trips* and *fixes,* but those who could afford it would take to drugs for no other reason perhaps than because it was anti-Establishment.

There was another thing about that lost generation of young people who were flailing about them in the street rallies and the demos., trying to establish for themselves a purpose and an identity. Most of them had grown up without religion, or had turned their backs upon the faith and convictions of their parents. What they were doing, in an aimless, frustrated and inconsequential fashion, was seeking out for new gods, other objects of worship, — and like the Children of Israel in their wanderings through the Sinai Desert, they would from time to time find themselves kneeling at the clay feet of graven idols. It was just another symptom of the humanistic revolution.

¶ 85 FAMOUS DRUG-TAKERS OF THE PAST

But the bearded drop-outs who filled the ranks of the Vietnam peace rallies, the groupies who shrieked themselves into hysteria at sight or sound of the Beatles, the kids who smoked reefers for kicks in the shaded lights of Saturday night discos, were not exactly top people. They must have provided the couriers and the pushers with a considerable amount of extra business, but most of them would draw back from experimentation with the harder drugs, and few would end up with an addiction. Also, theirs was an immature and transient flirtation, — scarcely likely to give the cult of drug-taking that accolade of acceptance and respectability at which we have been hinting.

So where in society past or present do we find a recognisable group of top people, — people of standing and influence, — who have favoured the use of drugs, and would instinctively resent measures taken by the authorities to ban their importation and distribution? Big names? Famous names? Names renowned and illustrious enough to command a following, even to inspire a new philosophy?

What about Havelock Ellis, the nineteenth century sexologist, mentor and collaborator of Sigmund Freud, and sometimes hailed as the father of social psychology? Ellis was an enthusiastic advocate of hallucinatory experiences, and experimented for this purpose with the drug peyote, which he was known to have imported from America. A founder of the Fabian Society, contemporary and colleague of George Bernard Shaw and the other leading lights of Bloomsbury socialism, he was neither selfish nor reticent about his depravities and addictions, sharing both the drugs and his esoteric experiences with chosen companions.

A subsequent recruit to this magic circle of psychopaths and deviants was the future economist John Maynard Keynes, who quickly warmed to the Ellis creed of self-justification for even the most perverted habit, and soon adapted it to cover perversions and idiosyncrasies of his own. When his homosexual partner Lytton Strachey took to smoking hashish, Keynes defended both him and his indulgence, just as George Bernard Shaw had done on an earlier occasion with Oscar Wilde.

Inspired by those giants of literature and economics who lived and dwelt among them, the Bloomsbury circle of early Fabians, atheists, agnostics and Marxist Internationalists clearly adopted a policy of "Anything goes!", and were willing both to conceal and to forgive every vice, perversion and depravity to which their luminaries were addicted. Many would seek to emulate them out of sheer affectation, and there in the heart of early twentieth century London a cult and a philosophy were being born which sought stimulation in the use of drugs, and regarded them as a source of ever more titillating experiences.

So! It was all before the days of the anti-narcotics branch, the drug-addiction clinics, and those pathetic Tv documentaries about kids who get hooked on heroin before they're old enough to know what life is all about. You might argue that the Bloomsbury set, with their hashish smoking, their sex perversions and their denigratory attitudes towards king, country and religion, were pandering to their own elitist tastes, and might conceivably have adopted a double standard to prevent their own peculiar indulgences from disseminating through the rest of society. In other words, did they really want to see the world populated with sex deviants and dope sufferers staggering through to the next fix?

¶ 86 THE LEAGUE OF SPIRITUAL DISCOVERY

Let us judge only by the record. And the record tells us that much of what John Maynard Keynes and Havelock Ellis and George Bernard Shaw thought in their own time was destined to flavour the customs and the attitudes of later generations. The Neo-American Church for instance, a sect of those Unitarian-Universalists who led the signing of the First Humanist Manifesto, regards drugs and drug-taking as an essential part of its services. It has enshrined the hallucinatory drugs peyote and mescaline as "sacred bio-chemicals", and protests that any effort to ban or restrict their use is an attack upon its religious freedom. Claire Chambers quotes the Neo-Americans from the pages of *The Humanist* as claiming that "everyone has the right to expand his consciousness and stimulate visionary experience by whatever means he considers desirable". So also, in his own time, said the sexologist Havelock Ellis.

The American Humanist Association does not reject its hallucinating clergy as naughty boys and delinquent brethren. In fact, looking forward to the day when private humanism will have assumed the mantle of a world religion, it seems to take the view that the psychedelic drugs like peyote, marijuana and LSD will then be in regular use by its members.

In the nineteen-sixties the leader of the LSD cult in the United States was an odd character called Dr. Timothy Leary. Dr. Leary had formed himself and his adherents into a League of Spiritual Discovery (L.S.D. for short), and though his antics must conceivably have inspired many a derisory chuckle in the uninitiated, humanists took him very seriously indeed. A leader of the Neo-American

Psychedelics and the Drug Scene

Church is quoted as regarding him "with the same special love and respect as was reserved by the early Christians for Jesus".

How's that for blasphemy? Apparently the American authorities did not share the reverence of Leary's co-religionists. When his passion for psychedelics via the drug syndrome put him outside the law, he was obliged to flee the country in 1970.

¶ 87 THE PEDIGREE OF THE UNITARIANS

You are now at liberty to wonder whether we're not being a bit hard on the humanists, treating them as the veritable Aunt Sallys of the fairground. Take a shy at them on sex, drugs, immorality, — and it's every time a coconut!

You may also wonder whether a group of people who have never really hit the headlines could wreak such havoc in our society as has been described in the preceding chapters. You have perhaps tended to regard them as a bunch of scholarly, retiring chaps who could always be expected to take a *moderate* well-reasoned point of view on everything from nuclear power to the choice of a new greenkeeper for the bowling club. All savoir-faire and unassuming manners! The types who get elected to management boards and standing committees with circumlocutive names and important-sounding functions! Somehow it's hard to regard them as inheritors of that broad atheistic and anarchistic movement which triumphed briefly in Paris at the time of the French Revolution, and thereafter persisted through secret societies and underground cells up to the commissioning of the Communist Manifesto in 1848; which in its turn threw together in Victorian London those middle-class revolutionaries Karl Marx and Frederich Engels, who between them created the climate of free thinking, sexual licence and subversive intrigue that would bring forth the satanically perverted genii of Havelock Ellis and John Maynard Keynes!

As we have seen, George Bernard Shaw was also of that intimate circle, and knew all there was to know about the morals, perversions, licentious living habits and global ambitions of his epoch-shattering contemporaries. Shaw became a living link between the Bloomsbury set, the London Fabians and the early Unitarians, who would claim to themselves the credit for having formed the

American Humanist Association.

Out of the Unitarians and their union with the Universalists would come the cult of religious humanism, which freely admitted to its membership and to its churches those of any faith, — or no faith at all. And out of the practice of religious humanism came the passion for psychedelics and hallucinatory experience-seeking which would make Dr. Timothy Leary the new Christ of the LSD cult in the United States.

¶ 88 ARE THESE THE PROTECTORS?

Is it all there? Is the continuity well-enough established? Those who accept the logic and the linking as it is briefly stated here can move on with us to the next deduction. The doubters and the frankly incredulous will please have the good grace and the integrity to study in fuller detail the great mass of evidence which is readily available,— some of it pridefully offered by the humanists themselves. The monumental work of research on the subject was done somewhere between 1974 and 1977 by the American Claire Chambers, whose painstaking exposure of *The SIECUS Circle* is noted in the bibliography.

We started out with an unanswered question about the vast illegal and immoral trade in narcotics, which is reputedly responsible for so much incidental crime and violence, and which commits the energy and resources of specialist police forces in Britain, Europe and America. We wondered at the helplessness of the authorities to do more than contain this trade, which feeds on rapacity, induced cravings and sheer human misery, — and we hinted that despite the well-publicised detestation of all decent people towards drugs and drug traffickers, there must surely be some influential segment of the population who were prepared to tolerate, even indulge them, — otherwise public revulsion would have eliminated them long ago.

In the Unitarians and the Universalists and their co-religionists in the Neo-American Church, have we found that important segment? And if we have, can it be said that they have power and influence enough to sustain a trade which is apparently abominated by the highest and the lowest in the land? All right, Timothy Leary, the high priest of LSD, got kicked out by the American authorities, and is no longer a factor to be reckoned with. But his views were never held in isolation. They were broadly supported by the executive directorate of the American Humanist Association, who saw in the psychedelic drugs "the true host of God" and the universal religion of the future.

¶ 89 A CAVALCADE OF HUMANIST POWER

Bit confusing, isn't it, with the bulk of us utterly abhorred by the evils and the potential miseries of drug addiction, whilst a prestigious and self-justifying pressure group, — a kind of state within a state, — provides a market and an aura of moral legitimacy for both the traffickers and the wretches they hold in thrall? Let's recapitulate on some of the V.I.P.'s who, — though not necessarily drug-takers themselves, — have marched, filtered or meandered through our previous chapters as they are seen to be working for humanist causes and conforming to humanist principles. Sir Julian Huxley, English professorial egghead who was just waiting around to be made the first director-general of UNESCO in 1946, and who had declared that humanism would be the next great religion of the future; Dag Hammarskjold, U.N. secretary general and lonely sexual deviate who played a leading part in most of the world body's apparently incomprehensible activities during the early years of its existence; U Thant, the Burmese humanist who succeeded him, and thereby ensured that humanist influences would retain control in that vital appointment; Eleanor Roosevelt, wife of America's wartime president, an insistent humanist voice within the White House, and herself totally involved in humanist causes; Walter Mondale, vice-president to Jimmy Carter, and for four years endowed with all the prestige and financial and manipulative muscle wielded by a supremely confident humanist lobby in its bid to take over the United States Government; John Dewey, the founding father of American Fabian-humanism, whose teachings would bear fruit unto the third and fourth generation; Dr. Mary Calderone, who as executive director of the unofficial and privately financed Sex Information and Educational Council, would in twelve short years bring about a virtual classroom revolution in American schools; John D. Rockefeller III, who as a child had been an early exposure to the Dewey teaching methods, and who grew up to become a leading advocate of Planned Parenthood, World Population Control and various other less publicised humanist aims and promotions.

Let's throw in a few more who may not have been previously mentioned, yet whose influence was no less potent in the imposition of humanist policies upon American, and subsequently and inevitably upon other Western societies; Arthur J. Goldberg, American representative to the U.N. in the nineteen sixties; Andrew Young, who held that same post for several years under Jimmy Carter; Dr. Eugene Carson Blake, chief administrative officer of the United Presbyterian Churches of America, and the man who once opined that the churches, under unified (humanist) leadership, might one day control the whole economy; Adlai Stevenson of the Americans for Democratic Action, whose own run for the presidency was unsuccessful, yet whose prestige as an egghead amongst Unitarian-Universalists would give credence and respectability to some of the less reputable causes which they were furtively promoting; Robert McNamara, long-time Chairman of the World Bank, and super-influential international humanist who got so carried away with the Rockefeller plans for zero population growth that he is reported to have threatened the withholding of loans from governments which did not introduce birth control programmes; H. R. Gaither, a former president of the Ford Foundation, who, as quoted by Claire Chambers, wanted *"to so alter American society that it could be comfortably merged with that of the Soviet Union"*.

You have to watch those taxfree American foundations because of the enormous funds which they have at their disposal; funds which mean power and helping hands and favourable media reporting for whatever bizarre and offbeat activity meets with their benign approval. When H. R. Gaither was at the Ford Foundation, it was listed as a major financial supporter of Dr. Mary Calderone's SIECUS organisation as it promoted sex education and "situation ethics" in schools. The Rockefeller Foundation and the Rockefeller Brothers Fund were prominent in the drive for World Population Control, and could always be relied upon for a sizeable donation to the Unitarian-Universalists in their long-term campaign to make universal humanism the psychedelically based, non-theistic religion of the future.

¶ 90 CAMPAIGN TO LEGALISE THE SOFT DRUGS

Get the message? Humanists help and endorse the aims and ideas of other humanists. They are also right in there at the pinnacles of the social, political and ecclesiastical power structure in both Britain and America, — and when it comes to something really big, with the Rockefeller family foundations behind them they have virtually all the money in the world at their disposal.

So in their attitude to drugs, — well, bearing in mind the strong public antipathies, they can't just afford to go overboard in direct support of their Unitarian and Neo-American brethren, who claim that any ban upon the use of peyote and mescaline is a restriction of their religious freedom. But what humanists *have* done is to put themselves and their wide resources solidly behind the campaign for legalisation of the so-called *soft* drugs such as marijuana and LSD. The subtle contention in support of this argument is that *soft* drug addiction only leads the user into *hard* drugs because, sharing their prohibited and illegal status, they become part of the same "criminal sub-culture". The deduction to be drawn from this novel theory is that once hemp and marijuana are legalised, they will lose their fascination for that segment of the population which gets its kicks by regularly bucking the law. They might then become the resort and the addiction of respectable members of society, who could hallucinate and go psychedelic without fear of prosecution.

Humanists do further maintain that *soft* drugs are no more dangerous or anti-social than the excessive consumption of alcohol,— a viewpoint which is fiercely resisted by the narcotics branches of police departments, who have statistics to show that "epileptic seizures, suicidal tendencies, successful suicides and even homicides" have been traced to the habitual use of LSD.

¶ 91 CHRISTIANS, STAND UP AND BE COUNTED!

So! getting to be too much of a good thing, this investigation of the humanists and their strange secular religion, which accepts virtually everything but a belief in Almighty God! Does it make you think of some headlines which the New York Times would never be allowed to print? *The Great Drug Scandal! Narcotics Racket fostered by the Advocates of Population Control! Humanists' Hearts Bleed for Victims of Heroin Addiction Whilst Their Soul Brothers Promote Mescaline and LSD!*

Finally of course, as with sex education and teenage violence, we find ourselves in the syndrome of the *Old One-Two,* where our reformist revolutionaries, having created the problem, are smart to come up with the solution.

And their solution to the drugs menace? Well, they've told us, haven't they? Just legalise the lot! Sell 'pot' and marijuana over the counter in the village shop along with the weekly groceries! Heroin and mescaline? Well, maybe you'll have to sign for these, and certify that they won't be on offer to an unregistered juvenile.

Sounds simple, doesn't it? But is that the kind of future society you want for yourself and your children? If it isn't, then for God's sake stand up and be counted in the battle against this atheistic creed which has already got a stranglehold upon the established churches, which dominates the policies of large institutions and multi-national corporations and even governments.

You're scared? It's too big for you? What can one person do when it's gone so far already? You'll be risking your job and your pension?

Friend, did you imagine that you were a Christian, — a real Christian, that is, untainted by humanist demonology? Well Christians in the past have never been reluctant to take up the unequal struggle, — and so often their faith has carried them through.

Do humanists intimidate you? Do they always sound so damned superior, with their logic and their rationalising, — and their insistence that everything has a materialist and a manmade explanation, from the Resurrection to the visitations of Lourdes?

Yet a pressing reason for the publication of this volume is to show the cesspit into which we will have descended if we ever allow humanist-materialist concepts to hold precedence over the Christian beliefs and ethical standards which have guided our race down through the ages.

Still reluctant to fight? Or is it just that you reckon you can safely leave it to the other fellow?

CHAPTER XI

¶ 92 A TOLERANCE OF OTHER FAITHS

It has been said that when people stop believing in God, they will start believing in anything. Kids who have been weaned away from churchgoing or Christian values by agnostic or hedonistic parents do not necessarily lose the instinct for worship. They simply transfer their idolatry to some manmade deity, such as a football player or a pop star. It is probably safe to say that few, if any, of the more fanatical 'groupies' who shrieked their adulation at Elvis Presley, or swooned on the footlights at the prospect of touching one of the fabulous Beatles, had ever felt the reverence of a House of God, or sensed that there were things beyond this life which mere mortals are not yet privileged to know.

We are not in business to enforce any particular doctrine, or to try and drag a whole generation of easy-going, moderate-minded but slightly irreverent folks back in fear and trembling of a jealous if unseen God. We need not, in fact, insist upon the exclusiveness of Christianity as the only true faith through which humanity can hope to gain salvation. There are, after all, other religions which have brought truth and love, discipline, orderliness and deep meaning into the lives of many millions of devout souls who never heard of the Sermon on the Mount or the sacrifice that was made nearly two thousand years ago on Calvary Hill.

Religion is belief, faith, — an understanding of the vastness of the cosmos, as something much greater than the minds and imaginations of mortal men. True religion becomes a way of life, a set of standards by which human beings can drag themselves upwards from the lusts and carnal appetites of the beasts of the field and jungle. If we talk here of the Christo-Judaic God, it is because devotion to that doctrine and set of beliefs has made Western civilisation what it is today. And since that is the established creed of the Anglo-Saxon, Celtic and Romance companies of nations, that is the faith with whose survival we are most concerned. It does not mean that Hindu, Jew, Buddhist and Muslim cannot live their lives side by side with us in tolerance. Those who have a faith, and who live devoutly by its tenets, can in the end only contribute to the sum of human happiness. Sometimes we can learn from their disciplines, and from the tradition and protocol which determines their way of life. Children of practising Muslims, for instance, do not graduate into porn or drug-taking, or form themselves into communes from which the family unit is excluded. Or do they?

¶ 93 PROLIFERATION OF WAY-OUT CULTS

Only the humanists claim to have a religion which makes man supreme, and which refuses to look beyond the limits and confines of this mortal existence for the elemental truths of life itself. They are careful not to discount the relevance of those other faiths, which sustained and uplifted humanity in more primitive days when it was struggling to overcome its environment. What they say is that such superstitious beliefs have now become *outmoded.* Man in his intellectual and technological achievements has *outgrown* them, as a growing child develops past his childhood toys.

Do *you* believe that, as you delve deeper into this catalogue of manmade confusion and disillusionment? Maybe you haven't had time to think about it, but is it not presumptuous to imagine that some nineteen hundred years of Christian culture, of faith and sacrifice, giving and enduring, of outstanding physical and mental achievement, can suddenly become *outmoded* because a group of inspired physicists have managed to split the atom, or the sophistications of rocket propulsion units have encouraged us to expect that we will one day reach the stars?

Man has not changed, even though his environment and his

expectations have changed. Individually or collectively, he is still small and insignificant in contemplation of the vast Universe that is all about us, and such is his nature that he can only feel truly secure in identification with Something which has its Being outwith the confines of self.

So when a generation sets out to live its life without the benefit of an established divinely based religion, it does not mean that there is *no* religion, — rather that religion and worship take on a number of bizarre manifestations. For with the diminishing of orthodox Christian belief, has there not been a corresponding proliferation of way-out sects, cults, strange rites and occultist practices? Remember what the man said, — *that when people stop believing in God, they start believing in anything.*

¶ 94 THE UNIFICATION CHURCH OF SUN MYUNG MOON

It might be some middle-aged jet-setting Messiah who has built himself a five million dollar pad on Long Island from the subscriptions of his faithful followers, — or an Oriental mystic such as the guru to whom the Beatles genuflected when, having made their fortunes out of the British pop scene, they became engrossed with an Eastern asceticism which seemed to offer them a whole host of new and exciting values that had somehow eluded them in the West.

It could be the hippie commune of the beastly Charles Manson, who surrounded himself with lissome female slaves, and lived off the dowries they brought with them from their well-heeled middle-class backgrounds. It might be the Unification Church of the Reverend Sun Myung Moon, which had built itself a considerable base in America, but which was conducting a brisk recruiting campaign through a number of British universities during the winter of 1978-79.

An initiation into the Moonie cult involves the immediate renunciation of all parental contact and guidance, and acceptance of the Reverend Moon as the true Father, both temporal and spiritual. Youngsters who become Moonies leave home and are housed in communal living quarters, where there is deliberate frustration of all attempts by their former families to reach them, either by word or letter. Moonification, or Unification, is apparently a sort of final play in the *generation gap* psychology which is the basis of humanistic teaching methods.

Parents who have lost their children to the Unification Church are generally reported to be in a terrible state of frustration and despair, and to be asking themselves what went wrong. You and I can tell them what went wrong, can't we? We can start by asking them where they were in their children's formative years. On the golf course? Or at protracted sessions in the bingo hall? Not preoccupied with the life and activities of the Church! That we can say for certain. Let's say that those distraught parents of a lost generation were good providers. The kids had warmth and congenial surroundings, and money to spend. They had a high school education, the prospect of a degree, and a job that befitted their qualifications. So where did those unhappy parents fail? What did they not do before sending their children out into the world? Just this! They had been unable, — or unwilling, — to imbue them with the deep and abiding faith which comes from a Christian upbringing. Like the humanists, whose doctrine and propaganda they had inadvertently swallowed, they had decided that such primitive beliefs were outmoded in this computerised technological age. They had taught their offspring a due and fitting reverence for the marvels of science, an awareness of man's genius in the control of his environment, in the perfection of communications and the conquest of disease. In all these respects they had prepared them to become the inheritors of the twenty-first century. But because they had not bothered to tell them that despite all these manmade wonders there was still a God in Heaven and a Holy Spirit that pervades all things, those precious children of theirs were wide open to temptation, and to the perversions of the Unification Church run by a truly irreverent gentleman called Sun Myung Moon.

¶ 95 JIM JONES AND HIS PEOPLE'S TEMPLE

Heard enough? Want some more examples of the heart sickness, the perverted yearnings, the sadistic impulses, the bestial abnormalities, the greed, rapacity and vain disillusioned searchings after purely mortal goals, which beset isolated and forlorn groups of confused humanity once the inspiring belief in a Supreme Being has been totally expunged from their lives?

What about *The People's Temple,* instituted in the 1950's in the American Mid West as a sort of pseudo-religious mission, attracting repressed minorities and drop-outs, performing social and charitable works which were initially financed by both public and private contributions? Its leader and founder was another of those self-styled reverends, Jim Jones, a man of great charisma and personality but no formal religious teaching, — and as latterly became all too well apparent, a demonic inspiration which was the very antithesis of Christ's function on earth.

This did not prevent him from claiming on occasions that he was Christ Re-incarnate, — a mantle which he assumed in contrast to his normal posture of the Marxist humanitarian, denouncing the Bible as a 'paper idol'. Get the pattern? The Reverend Jim Jones was a genuine derivative of the Humanistic Revolution, professing a pseudo-religiosity which hailed the Saviour Jesus Christ as the first Communist, and preaching a humanitarian mumbo-jumbo based on socialistic and revolutionary values, — adapting also a Satanic device utterly antagonistic to the Christian doctrine of love and tolerance, in that he drew many of his converts and adherents unto him by arousing the hate-filled spectre of a Mid-Western racial holocaust in which coloured folks would be suppressed and persecuted as were the Jews in Hitler's Germany.

Convinced by his own rantings, Jones finally departed the Mid-West with a nucleus of his followers to the comparative safety of California, where his Temple Headquarters were in due course established in San Francisco. There, in the spirit of the times, with humanistic concepts blurring public susceptibilities to a phony preacher who alternated with texts from the Communist Manifesto and the vision of a proletarian Christ Re-incarnate, Jones became a power in local politics, using the dedication of his Temple slaves to assist in the election of a mayor of the city, who reciprocated by making him Chief of the Housing Authority.

¶ 96 FRIENDS IN HIGH PLACES

The Reverend Jones had made the American Establishment.

And when the time came to elect born-again Jimmy Carter President of the United States, the founder of the People's Temple was honoured by a private chat with fellow humanist Walter Mondale, as well as appearing on the same public platform as First Lady Rosalynn, who was reported to be bewildered by the fact that 'the Rev.' commanded a much more enthusiastic following than herself. This aura of having friends in high places was to stand the cult leader in good stead when his Temple HQ was beset with allegations of graft and corruption, and illegal beatings and pressures being exerted on some of the initiates. It is reported that when these allegations were being investigated, influential political figures petitioned the Attorney's office, urging him to drop the enquiry. Well naturally! The Reverend Jim was one of the boys, wasn't he? preaching Marxist-socialist-humanism under the mantle of charitable religious evangelism, and knowing instinctively which side to be on next time political appointments were up for grabs.

But what with one thing and another, the founder of the People's Temple had decided that the future of his movement lay outside the United States. His vision of a racial holocaust in Indiana had changed to one of nuclear annihilation in California, and he told the faithful that the answer lay in a socialist retreat which he would prepare for them in some remote corner of the Earth. They were therefore urged to give generously and give often, so that he could build up the necessary finances for moving the whole organisation out to a Promised Land.

¶ 97 THE HELL COLONY OF JONESTOWN

When he finally started a new settlement in the former colony of British Guiana, — then converted into a Communist People's Democracy in the style so characteristic of the Fabian de-colonisers at the British Foreign Office, — he is reputed to have taken with him several million dollars in American cash and cheques, plus the bespoken remittances and social security entitlements of many of his thousand followers, who as a first article of faith were expected to turn over all their worldly wealth to the cause.

Clearing jungles, even to provide a tropical paradise and nuclear refuge, is very hard work, and while it's happening the work can become an end in itself. After it's over, folks have time to sit down and wonder about the purpose of it all, — and unfortunately the nuclear holocaust was refusing to arrive on schedule. Jones got up to all sorts of stunts, distracting, bizarre and spectacular, — all in an effort to keep his disciples in line, — but settling down to life in a hastily constructed jungle encampment must have presented difficulties for a community which came from a predominantly urban background. Discipline grew strict, and eventually repressive. Automatic weapons which had initially been imported into the commune as a pretext for defence against the C.I.A. or other such counter-revolutionary intruders, came in the end to be directed against the inmates themselves as Jonestown developed into a hell colony ruled by a fanatical paranoiac.

Matters came to a head in November of 1978 when, following up disquieting reports which had leaked out to the United States, a group of American newsmen and photographers led by a U.S. congressman called Leo J. Ryan flew into Guyana for an on-the-spot investigation. This visit, which began cordially enough, intensified the tensions within the colony to the extent that Jones was threatened with mass desertions as a number of the dissident settlers tried desperately to get on board the aircraft that were taking the congressman and his party back to the States.

On the morning of his departure Ryan and several of his companions were shot dead by commune guards at the nearby airstrip. Meanwhile the Satanic Messiah, founder of the People's Temple and of the socialist refuge of Jonestown, had ordered a mass suicide of all his followers in reprisal for this unwarranted outside interference. Hundreds of the more docile cultists, along with scores of innocent children, drank cyanide potions which killed them instantly. Many of those who resisted were gunned down by Jones's lieutenants, whilst others made a mad scramble to escape into the surrounding swamp and jungle. All in all, it was reckoned that some nine hundred people, including the cult founder and his wife and child, had died in that macabre nightmare of murder and suicide. And in his final hours preacher Jim Jones, self-styled Christ Re-incarnate, arbiter of life and death over several thousand deranged and pathetically mis-directed human beings, dictated letters to the

Russian Consul in Georgetown bequeathing all of the Temple's realisable assets to the Soviet Union, "because", he said, "we as Communists want our money to be of benefit for help to oppressed people all over the World".

¶ 98 RELATING IT BACK TO THE HUMANISTS

Bit of a tangle, isn't it? The Reverend Jim Jones was reckoned to be mentally deranged when he gave orders for the mass slaughter, but what of the others who followed him so blindly? Could it have happened in a society where God's word was strong, and where the clever people, the academics and the intellectuals, were not preaching a doctrine of man's self-sufficiency and potential to control all the things in his environment? Those poor misguided folks of San Francisco who gave their all for the mountebank Jim Jones were certainly not in charge of their environment. *They* had never had any illusions about their ability to cope with the pressures of life entirely alone. They were eager for some Higher Power which they could revere and respect, and to which they could look up for leadership. In seeking vainly for that outmoded Deity, they found Jim Jones instead, and went on from there to the dementia and slaughter of Jonestown.

Is it far-fetched to relate that macabre episode in Guyana back to those humanist smoothies who, in their various manifestos, so confidently declared that mankind no longer needed worship? Can we blame the rise and fall of the People's Temple on the eggheads like Julian Huxley and Bertrand Russell and John Maynard Keynes and Walter Mondale and Arthur Goldberg and Adlai Stevenson and Dr. Kinsey and John Dewey, — all those clever, clever guys who just *knew* that humanity had been on the wrong track those last nineteen hundred years, and that they alone had the answer? Can we blame them likewise for the Moonies and the hippies, the pathetic heroin addicts and the drop-outs, the kids who become alienated from their parents?

O.k. I'm not *telling* you. I'm just asking you to think about it.

CHAPTER XII

¶ 99 JIMMY CARTER AND HUMAN RIGHTS

Perhaps the most heart-rending and potentially demoralising of many devious humanistic ploys has been their campaign on human rights. Whether they themselves coined the phrase and initiated the whole idealistic project, may be a matter for argument. What principally concerns us here is the manner in which a pursuit of human rights has been used to mask the long-term attainment of other less universally acceptable objectives. With their word-play upon things human, humane and humanitarian, the humanists have been able to perform a con. trick against Western society. There used to be an old Scots proverb which said that if you got the name of rising early, you could often get away with staying in bed till noon. So it has proved with the humanists. Having adopted some pretentious phrases and a number of idealistic causes, they have simply usurped the moral conscience of mankind, and used it as a cloak behind which to pursue their own globalistic ambitions.

The election of Jimmy Carter to the U.S. Presidency sparked off a veritable explosion in human rights activity. Carter himself was reported to be a "born-again Christian", whatever that may mean, — but in Walter Mondale he had a prominent East Coast Establishment humanist as his vice-president, and in Andrew Young a Marxist ambassador to the United Nations. So in these two appointments alone he showed himself to be a type of social-gospelling churchman who could always enter into a dialogue with materialism.

This notwithstanding, his apparently uncompromising stand on human rights earned him wide support amongst the Christian communities of Europe and America, where it had generally been assumed that the most atrocious assaults upon human dignity and the freedom of the individual were still being perpetrated in that vast empire of Russian, Slavonic and satellite states controlled by the Soviet Union. The purges and the show trials of Stalin's day had given way to more subtle methods of enforcing the Communist ethic, and the counter revolutionaries, reactionaries and deviationists of that earlier era had been phased out, — to be replaced by a new generation of intellectual, moral and religious 'dissidents', men and women who somehow found extraordinary courage and resolve with which to confront the terror apparatus of the Politburo and the KGB.

It had been to the undying shame of Western peoples and their governments that, — largely through humanistic influences, — they had failed to respond to the shining example of those modern martyrs, and had allowed them to sink into the oblivion of Siberian penal colonies or Muscovite psychiatric clinics, where the breaking of their minds and bodies could proceed at a leisurely pace isolated from public notice. So if Jimmy Carter, freshly appointed as Chief Executive of the Western World's most powerful nation, was prepared to backtrack upon that disgusting catalogue of shame and pusillanimity, there might still be hope for some of those brave individuals who had given their all to demonstrate that even under the most draconian tortures there is something in the greatness of the human soul which cannot be utterly extinguished. Many millions of Christian people wished him well.

¶ 100 NO RELIEF FOR THE RUSSIAN DISSIDENTS

History is now able to evaluate the results of that Carter Human Rights Campaign, which finally foundered round about the time of the Russian invasion of Afghanistan. Expensively run, high-powered committees and commissions set up an almost continuous dialogue, in which the Soviets, as might have been expected, parried all investigations and criticisms through the bland expertise of their most experienced prevaricators. And the persecution of 'dissidents' went on without visible interruption. Alexander Ginzburg was sentenced to eight years in a "special regime" labour camp for anti-Soviet propaganda in July of 1978, and human rights crusader Anatoli Shcharansky, who had possibly become emboldened by the promised American initiatives, got thirteen years in prison and labour camps, allegedly for conveying information to Western sources about Soviet defence and scientific research establishments.

Other cases did not involve the same political overtones. The Russian baptist Georgi Vins was still serving out the ten years of prison and exile imposed upon him in 1975 entirely because of his religious convictions, and there was unrelenting pressure and persecution of all fundamentalist sects and breakaway Christian groupings who had rejected the official religious orthodoxies favoured by the state. Dr. Andrei Sakharov continued his hazardous political tight-rope walking under the very noses of the KGB and the Soviet authorities, — and as we were to learn from men like Vladimir Bukovsky, who came over to the West in 1976, the entire Russian economy had come to depend upon a permanent convict population of some two and a half million people, deliberately kept on a starvation diet and used as forced labour on construction projects in many of the remote and climatically severe regions of the U.S.S.R.

Human rights? There appeared to be such a total disregard of basic humanitarian instincts in the ethos of the Russian Communist system as to occupy, immerse and consume a whole army of human rights activists for the duration of their natural lives. Even so, after shattering a few of their lances against the shield of Soviet obduracy, the Carter campaigners became discouraged, and started looking around for easier fields to conquer.

¶ 101 PRESSURES ON IRAN, CHILE AND NICARAGUA

They found it much easier to make progress in Southern Africa, and in places like Iran, which was still a sphere of American influence. There the new Carter policy of pursuing human rights to the exclusion of political strategy resulted in the eventual collapse of the Shah, de-stabilisation of the entire Persian Gulf region, a Russian advance into Afghanistan, and further inflationary upsurges in the crude oil market.

In South America the Carter approach would be contradictory, and equally disastrous for American strategic interests. He was to sustain and encourage, both morally and financially, the repressive regime of Panamanian dictator Omar Torrijos, whilst at the same time throwing the full weight of American diplomatic disapproval against Pinochet in Chile, and Somoza in Nicaragua. Pinochet, who braved the hazards and uncertainties of a popular vote in a referendum, emerged victorious and managed to hold his government together despite American hostility. But Somoza, fighting a virtual civil war against the Sandinista guerrillas, financed and armed by Fidel Castro of Cuba, and supplied via neighbouring Costa Rica, was to complain that he had been forced into surrender by economic sanctions and an arms embargo controlled and orchestrated from Washington, D.C.

¶ 102 A SPRINGBOARD FOR COMMUNIST EXPANSIONISM

All right! so the Carter Human Rights Campaign had won through to total success in at least one South American country. This fellow Somoza sounded like a read bad 'un, since it seemed that the Organisation of American States, the Soviet Union, Fidel Castro, Omar Torrijos, the Sandinista guerrillas and the assorted communications networks of Britain and the United States all wanted rid of him. So what had he done to make him such a monster? Did he torture and execute his political opposition, as did Torrijos in nearby Panama? Did he stage show trials and lock up 'dissidents' in concentration camps and penal colonies, as did the Soviets in Russia? Did he connive at cannibalism, as did the self-styled Emperor of the Central African Republic? or personally participate in ritualistic beatings, like Idi Amin in Uganda? Friend! if you relied upon the popular press and the Tv networks, you would be quite unable to answer any of these questions, for they simply did not tell you. Somoza was bad because they *said* he was bad, — and that was all you were expected to know about the subject. The fact that he was a former graduate of West Point, an anti-communist and a stout ally of American foreign policy was almost obscenely irrelevant. So

Nicaragua got its Sandinista revolution, and a graphic re-run of the arbitrary arrests and summary executions which had characterised the Torrijos conquest of Panama some ten years previously.

It also provided a valuable springboard for an extension of Communist hegemony over a strategic area which had formerly been almost exclusively an American preserve. Ever look at Nicaragua on the map? It sits in the centre of that isthmus which from Panama to Mexico links together the two great sub-continents of the Americas. If Jimmy Carter had won the 1980 presidential election, it would have been a stepping stone to the further conquests of El Salvador and Guatemala, both troubled by civil strife and armed insurrections, and both potential targets for the Carter human rights crusaders. Then it only needed the isolation of Honduras and the absorption of Belize and Costa Rica to provide Cuba's Communist dictator with a whole string of potential allies from north to south of the Panamanian isthmus.

Wonderful what can be done with human rights! Over the four years of the Carter presidency, his campaign had failed to free even a single Russian 'dissident'. Neither had it encroached upon the brutally repressive regimes in Cambodia, Panama and Uganda. But it had further eroded the substance and the resolve of those states and nations which in Africa, Asia and South America continued to take a firm line against Communist subversion.

There are many contradictory considerations which prey upon the executive of a great nation, and go to the final formulation of national policy. Some of them may be repugnant to particular presidents and prime ministers, yet be forced upon them by the exigencies of the moment. But in the matter of Jimmy Carter's human rights campaign of 1976-80, and the bias that it developed, it is difficult to escape the conclusion that its most notable failure and some of its successes were pre-destined from the beginning, *and that the influential humanist elements within the Carter Administration were working furtively towards that goal which had been stated for them by H. R. Gaither, some time of the Ford Foundation, when he confessed that a primary objective of institutional policy was "so to alter American society that it could be comfortably merged with that of the Soviet Union"*.

¶ 103 WHY HAS THE WCC FAILED TO HELP THE NEW RUSSIAN MARTYRS?

So much for the political side of human rights, which has been seen to have its pragmatic limitations! What then of the ecclesiastical? After all, there had been a representative world church organisation since 1948, and though this was initially an ecumenical convocation of Protestants and Anglicans from Europe and America, it would subsequently widen its scope and its articles to incorporate all the major world churches, including those of Eastern Europe and Soviet Russia.

Bravo for our crusaders in clericals, you might say! When they admitted the Moscow Patriarchate of the Russian Orthodox Church into their councils in 1961, they had surely created a vehicle whereby all forms of religious and social persecution might be exposed and ventilated. At this stage those who remember the unshakeable faith and stoical courage of Hungary's Cardinal Mindszenty might conjure up visions of black-bearded Russian patriarchs jet-flighting to Western capitals to commune with their brethren from the brighter side of the Iron Curtain on matters concerning freedom of thought and religious observance for the flocks which they had left behind them in Smolensk or Stalingrad or Nijni Novgorod. A progressive breakdown of the repressive Soviet system through the single-minded devotion of God-fearing Orthodox priests as they defied the Kremlin and its materialist ideology to join in an impressive demonstration of Christian unity! The souls of the tortured and the living dead uplifted even in the midst of their privations by the knowledge that through their clergy they once again had access to a free society where moral and diplomatic pressures could be brought to bear! Onward Christian soldiers! New hope and salvation under the blessed Sign of the Cross!

Is that it? Is that how we might have been expected to welcome the news that the WCC had somehow managed to persuade atheistic Communism to relax its prejudices and soften its iconoclasm by allowing its religious dissenters to bear a true Christian witness within the bosom of a restored Mother Church?

If so, what went wrong? Why is it that after twenty years of committees and conferences, during which Russian and Eastern European ecclesiasts have sat down many times with their Western colleagues to discuss the Church's mission in this modern age, so little has been said and done to ease the persecution of Russia's Christian martyrs? Why so little mention of the ruthless terror unleashed against Jehovah's Witnesses, Pentecostalists and Ukrainian Baptists in an effort to make them fit into the mould of communist conformity? Why no Christian witness at the show trials of men like Alexander Ginzburg and Anatoli Shcharansky and Viktoras Petkus? Why no reports by the Moscow Patriarchate upon the Soviet penal system, which, according to Vladimir Bukovsky, kept a permanent convict population of over two million people on forced labour and a starvation diet?

¶ 104 FRERE YAKUNIN'S LETTER

Why? why? why? Well the charitably-minded might argue that those Russian Orthodox churchmen who sat on the Central Committee of the WCC had got their passports and their visas on suffrance, that they had not been allowed to forget the realities of life within an atheistic authoritarian dictatorship, and that any human rights crusading on their part which embarrassed the Soviet Government, or dented its image abroad, would meet with swift reprisals and a clamp down on future contacts.

All right! those of us who have never experienced Communist vengeance at first hand can well imagine that tne threat of long-term incarceration in a Soviet slave labour camp or Siberian salt mine would quench the boldest spirit, quell the bravest heart. But this is not the sort of thing we have come to expect of Christ's missionaries down through the ages. Always it has seemed that faith gave men a special kind of courage, even in the face of hopeless odds and draconian tortures. So what was the quality which inspired the Ginzburgs and the Shcharanskys and the Petkuses, but which was somehow lacking in those representatives of the Russian Orthodox Church who sat upon the Central Committee of the World Council of Churches, and who from their strategic positions could have done so much to expose the plight and alleviate the sufferings of those who were being persecuted for their faith within the Soviet Union?

In "The Fraudulent Gospel" Bernard Smith makes mention of a letter which had been smuggled out of the U.S.S.R. in time for the WCC's Nairobi Assembly, and which shed some light upon the attitudes and motives of the official Russian delegation. Written by two members of the Orthodox Church, a priest and a layman, this letter was published in full in the Assembly's daily news sheet, and was therefore brought to the notice of the entire conference. It stated that the "believers of the Russian Church never had any particular illusions about the fact that the Moscow Patriarchate became a member of the WCC: *it was an act sanctioned by the government during a period of extremely brutal persecution of religion,* and obviously followed the government's own strategic aims, which had nothing to do with the task of consolidating Christian positions in the modern world".

What do you make of that? Frere Yakunin, co-author of the smuggled letter, was himself one of those clergymen persecuted for their faith, — he had been deprived of his living for criticising the church leadership in its servility to the state. Now, with ingenious timing and publicity, his complaints had been laid before the whole WCC Assembly, and it was impossible for anyone to ignore the fact that it had happened.

¶ 105 FURY OF RUSSIA'S WCC DELEGATES UNDER CRITICISM

An act sanctioned by the government during a period of extremely brutal persecution of religion! Frere Yakunin and his lay colleague asserted that in the very year when the Russian Orthodox joined the WCC, there was a spate of anti-religious terror, marked by the "forcible closing of churches, monasteries and theological schools everywhere".

So in such circumstances, what kind of men were those church dignitaries who, with official Kremlin backing, went forward to represent the religious life of their country? Political priests? government stooges? wolves in sheep's clothing? It was subsequently reported by a British delegate, the Reverend Richard Holloway, that whilst the Yakunin letter was being angrily and noisily debated at the Nairobi Assembly, he found one of the furious Russian delegation to be "a KGB agent masquerading as a Baptist minister".

That tells us a great deal, doesn't it? We have now unearthed a significant truth, which will be promptly snatched and obfuscated away unless we cling to it tenaciously whilst it is in our hands, — that the East European delegation to the Central Committee of the WCC was *not* composed of stalwart Orthodox patriarchs created in the mould of Cardinal Mindszenty, that those of them who survived the Stalinist purges had been replaced by Muscovite hard men vetted by the Politburo, and briefed to further the strategic aims of the Soviet Government.

If, therefore, you were to ask your own church's WCC delegate why the Nairobi Assembly did not institute a searching investigation into the persecution of Russia's Christian groupings after debating the Yakunin letter, he would tell you that as a consequence of admitting the politically motivated East Europeans to the Central Committee, the preponderance of voting power within the World Council had now swung heavily in favour of the Soviets and their allies in Third World countries, who could normally be depended upon to follow the Communist party line. This meant an implied embargo on all criticisms of what was going on within the U.S.S.R., so there was understandable fury and a sense of outrage amongst the Russian delegation when Frere Yakunin's remonstrances were brought to the notice of the Assembly.

It is recorded that a Swiss delegate eventually managed to put down a motion showing concern about restrictions to religious liberty, *particularly within the U.S.S.R.,* and requesting the U.S.S.R. Government to implement the relevant principles of the Helsinki Agreement. Following some discussion, the motion was then referred back to Committee, and when it was put forward for ratification the next morning, *all references to the U.S.S.R. had been carefully deleted.*

So! Brave men, Frere Yakunin and his lay colleague Lev Regelson! Knowing, as they did, the political composition of the Moscow Patriarchate, they were probably not unduly surprised that their gallant gesture in smuggling that critical letter out to the Nairobi Assembly had failed to achieve its principal objective anent the persecution of Russia's religious minorities. But were they not entitled to expect a more spirited reaction from the Protestant Churches of the West, who, outvoted as they might be, surely felt that now, as never before, they had to be the torchbearers for all of Christendom?

¶ 106 WHO MENTIONED A CONFESSION OF FAITH?

Friend or fellow Christian! we seem to have let slip one or two significant observations on that subject already. The original World Council of Churches, as constituted in 1948, was presumably formed as an amalgamation or an offspring of the various national councils of churches in Europe and America. One of its principal aims was to hasten the development of the ecumenical movement, which aspired to an elimination of the differences and divisions in worship, firstly between Protestant denominations, and latterly between them and Roman Catholicism. Those ecclesiastical administrators who put together the organisation of the WCC may not have wasted time and energy broadcasting their intentions, but there is no doubt that their eventual purpose was the creation of a universal church, — a truly global church so broadly based in its doctrine and so tolerant in its interpretation of moral and religious values that it could freely admit within its doors people of all faiths, equally with those who had no faith at all.

Therefore when the opportunity came to admit delegations from the communised countries of Eastern Europe, the emphasis was all on globalism and upon the enhanced prestige and authority which the enlarged organisation was likely to command, rather than upon the concern for Christian standards and a revival of Christian belief in those lands where there now was a degree of formal representation. Obviously there was no requirement for a Confession of Faith before the new men from the Russian Orthodox Church took their places on the WCC Central Committee. If there had been, it would have created a few flutters and heartsearchings amongst the Western delegations as well, since those of them who graduated through the Unitarian and Universalist Churches had already got to the top of the ecclesiastical hierarchy without betraying any reverence for the teachings of Jesus Christ or His promises of a life hereafter. Remember the assertion of a past director of the American Humanist Association that it had grown out of Unitarianism as a movement of religious humanists, and that no less than 170 Unitarian-Universalist ministers were signatories to the Second Humanist Manifesto of 1973.

After all that, who would you reckon to wield the preponderating influence within the councils of the WCC? This author has had neither time nor opportunity to search out individual members of delegations and sound them on the spiritual quality or otherwise of their beliefs and motivations. But it is surely quite clear from its policies, and the manner in which it distributes its funds and its exhortations, that collectively this global church is a purely humanist conception which devotes itself principally to humanist aims and purposes, that it is ideologically more attuned to Marxist materialism and globalist concepts than it is to individual thought and freedom of conscience, — and that those who suffer pain and degradation for their religious beliefs on whatever side of the Iron Curtain, have as much hope of redress and protection at the hands of the WCC as a canary infatuated with the family cat, or a fox at a foxhunters ball.

The prevailing theme of this volume thus far has been to show the disintegrating effects upon our institutions, our educational system and our social and family life when Christians enter into a dialogue with humanism and its twin philosophy of communist materialism. We can now take a look at some of the brutal, bestial and atrocious things which happen to our world when secular humanism takes over the funds and functions of the mission church.

CHAPTER XIII

¶ 107 THE PROGRAMME TO COMBAT RACISM

As was illustrated in the previous chapter, the Central Committee of the WCC has now become a lopsided body, with its bias permanently slanted in the one direction. Due to the preponderance of voting power at the disposal of the Russians and their Third World allies, it is impossible to put through any motions or policy enactments which are in any way critical of the Soviet Union. On those few occasions when individual Western delegates manage to focus some attention upon abuses of human rights within the Communist system, they are countered by stonewalling on the part of the East Europeans, who will rise one by one, with their hands on their hearts, and swear vehemently that there is no such thing as a denial of human rights anywhere inside their respective countries.

On the other hand, where there is consideration of suppression, discrimination or social injustice in various parts of the non-communist world, the Central Committee has normally been able to progress its business with active cooperation and a high degree of unanimity all round. Millions who had never even heard of the WCC were to have their lives irretrievably altered by its initiation in 1969 of a Programme to Combat Racism. This was implemented through the creation of a special fund which the Committee in its wisdom would allocate to various parts of the underdeveloped world where there was internal strife as between racial and tribal groupings and their governments. In effect it meant giving considerable sums of money to a number of guerrilla armies and "liberation" movements in South America and Southern Africa.

The first allocation was about 200,000 American dollars, and after that there were annual disbursements till by 1981 the donors at the WCC had handed out to so-called anti-racist groups a total well in excess of two million dollars. With each disbursement it was emphasised that the money was intended for purely humanitarian purposes, for the supply of medicines and comforts, for the relief of suffering amongst women and children left destitute by scorched earth tactics or reprisals in the midst of guerilla war.

A laudable purpose, you might think! It would not be the first time the mission church had moved in on a scene of human conflict, dispensing aid and comfort and medical assistance with fine impartiality to all in need, irrespective of creed or colour. Only in this instance there did not seem to be a spirit of true impartiality. The commissioners of the WCC in too many cases were forming their own judgments, deciding upon the rights and wrongs of political and racial questions, and showing a disturbing tendency to side instinctively with the subversive, the revolutionary, the Marxist ideologist who wanted to destroy the entire structure of indigenous society. Also, it was freely admitted that once the money had been handed over, there was no control over the manner in which it might be spent. In a guerrilla context, even food and fuel must be regarded as part of the logistics of war, and governments who claimed for themselves a certain legitimacy through the ballot box, who were also trying to be responsible for the safety and welfare of all their population, felt justifiably aggrieved that rebellion within their borders was being fostered and encouraged by such a morally impressive body as the World Council of Churches.

¶ 108 RENDERING UNTO CAESAR

If, as political animals, we are asked to take a broad look at the many governments, elected or otherwise, — the regimes, absolute monarchies, sheikhdoms, despotisms and proletarian dictatorships which administrate, and sometimes repress and manipulate, the diverse peoples and populations who inhabit the Earth, — how, and by what criteria, are we to judge which of them should be supported, which should be marked down for future upheaval and dissolution?

Right away we are confronted by our own prejudices. The monarchists amongst us will tend to favour those hereditary rulers who inherit their absolutist powers from an illustrious past, — and who, in the ideal, are taken to be exercising their princely prerogatives for the benefit of all the people. Democrats, of whatever creed or colour, must by principle accept the occasionally capricious verdicts of the ballot, — provided this is recorded by free electorates under neither restraint nor intimidation. Democratic libertarians may also feel obliged to organise and campaign for a world in which *all* peoples, — at *all* stages of development, — can effectively sustain or depose their rulers by a system of universal suffrage. Anarchists will subscribe to the overthrow and destruction of all governments, wheresoever they might be found, — and pragmatists who understand the limitations of popular wisdom will opt generally for a preservation of order and civilised standards, even at the expense of some measure of human freedom.

But what should be the attitude and involvement of the Church in such matters? Jesus Christ began His mission on Earth under an Imperial rule which many must have regarded as repressive and unjustly biased against their national aspirations. When asked the loaded question, He is reported to have replied, "Render unto Caesar that which is Caesar's". In His profound understanding and spiritual serenity, He had turned aside any challenge to the powers and legitimacy of the State, and had concentrated the minds of His disciples upon the eternal values. In later centuries, as the Church became institutionalised, it departed from the Christian ideal on more than one occasion, conniving at the overthrow of kings and princes, and setting up various forms of ecclesiastical government. Come the Reformation, a new style of religious rivalry developed, whereby the traditionalists of the papacy, and even denominational groupings of the Reformed Church, gave their blessing and their sponsorship to bloody conflicts which would determine whose influence was paramount in parliament or at court.

So those who forecast an end to moral and religious strife through the Humanist Manifesto and the Universal Church were at least entitled to a hearing. Perhaps in the beginning there were few with sufficient prescience and fundamental commitment to spot the pitfalls and the fallacies, and in general a Church which could be seen to function without prejudices, internecine conflict and differences of doctrine and belief, was bound to have a nigh irresistible attraction for that great majority of human beings whose principal desire is to live at peace with their neighbours and their consciences.

The objective of this volume is not to blunt the aims or spurn the idealism of the true reformer, but rather to expose the traumatic implications of a globalist reform movement which has taken upon itself vast powers of patronage and dispensation, — and which, lacking that divine quality which alone could have ensured impartiality and justification, — has grievously lost its way.

¶ 109 PANDERING TO THE MARXISTS

In his story of how Nicaragua fell to the assault of the Sandinistas, the former President Anastasio Somoza tells how the revolutionary turmoil began in his country with the arrival of Jesuit priests who preached Communism to the sons and daughters of upper class families, and indoctrinated them into favouring the rebel cause. Jesuits! Devotees of the centuries-old Society of Jesus! Preaching Communism to the sons of Nicaraguan aristocrats and businessmen! Teaching them perhaps that Dialectic Materialism was the only true god, and that Karl Marx was its prophet!

Political priests! sent to prepare the ground for a Communist takeover in a strategic Central American state. Have we not been incredibly slow to realise what is happening, as those revolutionaries in clerical clothing set up a dialogue with Marxism which results eventually in the establishment of Cuban-style dictatorships inimical to the West?

In Southern Africa, where under its Programme to Combat Racism, the WCC was making annual disbursements of funds to assist guerrilla organisations in their campaign to overthrow white-ruled governments, the emphasis would again be on those with an ideological attachment to Marxism, and ambitions for a political system modelled upon that of the Soviet Union. ZANU and ZAPU guerrilla armies in what was then the state of Rhodesia! Frelimo in Mozambique! SWAPO in the former German South-West Africa, where an arrogant Sam Nujoma refused to accept any form of constitutional settlement, and demanded that power be handed over to him completely!

Though there might be any number of Christian-based organisations who campaigned for peaceful change and racial partnership, the WCC money seemed to be channelled almost exclusively towards the ideological Marxists who, with a plentiful supply of Russian arms, were waging campaigns of terror and intimidation in their respective countries, burning down kraals and isolated homesteads, closing down mission schools and deporting their black pupils to base camps in Zambia and Tanzania. It was as though the punters of the WCC Central Committee had already picked the likely winners in this macabre contest, and were hastening to place their investments with a view to future preference.

Might it be, in fact, that those globally-minded ecclesiasts, having shrewdly anticipated that the Marxist guerrillas of today were destined to become the presidents and prime ministers of tomorrow, had decided to cultivate their favours and earn their confidence, on the basis that they would deal more considerately with the Christian flocks who would fall under their domination once the independence wars were over?

¶ 110 THE TESTAMENT OF FATHER LEWIS

Father Arthur Lewis, an Anglican priest who for nine years served as pastor to a mission church at Mandea on Rhodesia's eastern border, and who was himself an eye-witness to the social disintegration and material destruction left behind by the guerrilla war, takes a dramatically different viewpoint. In "Christian Terror" he infers that the WCC was not so much a concerned bystander as a primary agent in the strife that engulfed Rhodesia, and that if the Churches had spoken out resolutely against terrorism in the first place, there would not have been any war.

"The churchmen," he says, "would then have had the opportunity to act as peacemakers, telling other countries to stay out and appealing for reconciliation and recognition on the basis of the overwhelming measure of agreement already reached between Rhodesian blacks and whites in 1961. . . . how many people remember that agreement *was* achieved at that time, only to be sabotaged by the intransigence of British governments backed by the British Council of Churches?"

A bit of near-forgotten history! but not the conventionally accepted view of what was happening about Rhodesia in the years before U.D.I.! An Anglican priest, — one who had given twenty years of his life to the spiritual, educational and material welfare of the rural African, — who spoke four native languages, and must surely have established some rapport with his black parishioners, — hinting that not only politics and politicians were involved in the many efforts to achieve a Rhodesian constitutional settlement, but that the ecclesiasts of the Universal Church had taken a hand in the proceedings, and their influence was largely malevolent!

All right! Father Lewis may never be invited to spread the Christmas message from the pulpit of St. Paul's Cathedral. In fact it may be that he will have difficulty in finding a pulpit from which he can preach at all. This is not because of any lack of dedication in his pastoral mission, any scandal or shortcoming in his personal life, any heresy of doctrine or interpretation of the faith, which might have made the Church justifiably wary of continuing or extending his licence.

Quite the reverse, as it happens! Arthur Lewis's speeches and writings reveal him to be utterly committed on biblical truth, and upon the fundamental teachings passed down to us by Jesus Christ. Very much an orthodox Anglican clergyman who, had he chosen to lead his life differently, might have become the universally respected upholder of the faith in some idyllic English village! Instead of which, he was to see his pastoral charge in rural Africa destroyed by bloody terrorism, — and to face growing opposition within his own hierarchy for his outspoken criticisms of those things which he regarded as a corruption of the Church's mission on earth.

¶ 111 THE PRIEST WHO WOULD NOT COMPROMISE

So what goes wrong when a dedicated God-fearing clergyman like Father Arthur Lewis finds himself totally at variance with the entire ecclesiastical establishment? Who or what was to blame? Was it personality, paranoia, rigidity of doctrine, — or a reluctance to face up to changing conditions?

Certainly in one respect Lewis had refused to move with the times. He had refused, on any pretext, or under any consideration, to enter into a dialogue with Marxism. To him the absolute values of the divine faith could not be reconciled with a creed and an ideology whose standards were relative and subject to the expediency of the moment. He made no secret of his belief that the eventual policy of the World Council of Churches was to establish a form of Christo-Marxism under which the earth-bound philosophy of the nineteenth century revolutionary would tend progressively to supersede the eternal teachings of the Man who died on Calvary.

For *Marxism,* of course, you and I could substitute the word *humanism,* and when we do so, it is seen that Father Lewis is cutting very close to the bone. Remember that the original impetus towards world ecumenicalism was provided by the Unitarians who, according to Edwin H. Wilson, founded the American Humanist Association "as a movement of religious humanists", and that Unitarian-Universalist churches freely accept members of all faiths, as well as those who have no faith at all.

So the orthodox conceptions of the Anglican priest from the Mandea Mission were probably regarded as an obstacle to his advancement in a World Church hierarchy which had long ago downgraded the Sermon on the Mount in favour of the Communist Manifesto. Also, his earlier exposure of political indoctrination at a farm cooperative on the Rusape Mission in the Diocese of Mashonaland had resulted in embarrassing questions being asked about church involvement with the African National Congress. How then were the advocates of Christo-Marxism to deal with this turbulent priest who would admit no compromise in his interpretation of the faith, and who went on insisting that Jesus was Lord of all?

¶ 112 BANNED FROM HIS NATIVE SHORES

In May of 1977, at the Synod of the Diocese, questions were asked about his active participation in a non-sectarian organisation called the Rhodesia Christian Group, which Father Lewis had founded in order to establish contact across the denominational barriers with those who retained the same orthodox beliefs as his own. Some of his fellow Anglicans were anxious to make it clear that when he spoke for the RCG he did not necessarily speak for the Anglican Church, and though on that occasion the President of the Synod respected his right to freedom of speech, there were others less scrupulous in their desire to silence inconvenient opinion.

Towards the end of 1978 Arthur Lewis was in correspondence with the British Foreign and Commonwealth Office concerning his continued right, as a minister of religion, to circumvent the passport and travel restrictions imposed in 1968 by George Thomson against citizens of Ian Smith's Rhodesia. He had been invited by friends and adherents in the United Kingdom to come and tell them at first hand what was happening to the Christian Church under the stresses and brutalities of the guerrilla war, and in the circumstances it was an invitation which he would have been most reluctant to refuse.

But in January of 1979 he received official notification from London that his travel facilities had been withdrawn, that his preachings and writings had been interpreted by the Secretary of State as having "furthered or encouraged the unlawful actions of the illegal regime", and that he was in effect a prohibited immigrant to the land of his birth and Christian upbringing.

A strange state of affairs! Did Father Lewis plan to threaten the Queen, plant bombs in public places, demonstrate against the Government or assassinate the staff of foreign embassies under our protection, — as did other visitors to our shores, towards whom the mandarins at the Foreign and Commonwealth Office could at times become positively benevolent? Not really! Everyone knew that he was as traditionally English as Nelson's column, — that his visit, had it been allowed, would have been as decorous and as law-abiding as any parsons' outing, that his loyalty to our institutions and way of life was profound and utterly unquestionable, and that any system of state security which banned such a devout personality whilst freely admitting terrorists and enemies of the Queen's peace, was perverse to the point of lunacy.

So whence had the pressures come? Where in the British Establishment were there those who stood to be confounded and embarrassed by what Father Lewis had to tell? Let us assume that the bureaucrats at the Foreign and Commonwealth Office were merely concerned with the enforcement of regulations, and that someone had to interpret for them the manner in which the one-time Archdeacon of Inyanga had failed to meet their conditions. Despite his sympathy with many of the aims and actions of the Smith Government, he was essentially a religious figure, — not political, — and could only be expected to preach and lecture with authority upon matters that came within his own ecclesiastical experience. So who was it that wanted to cramp his style, shut him up, prevent him from giving his fellow Anglicans in Great Britain a first-hand account of what was happening to their mission church out there in the blood-stained Rhodesian bush? Which of our august institutions was likely to shy at the prospect of his using an English pulpit from which to condemn WCC financial support for a purely materialistic philosophy which had persecuted Christians and destroyed Christian standards wherever it was allowed to triumph, and which — so he felt, — would surely do so again if allowed to triumph in Rhodesia?

We do not know at this stage what Father Lewis might actually have said. The important thing in any case is not so much what he intended to say as the fact that he was prevented from saying it. Christians down through two millennia had defended the rights of others to speak their minds, even if it was only to utter a blasphemy. Could it be that there were those in the British Council of Churches who regarded this as a Voltairian absurdity, and who, having guilty minds about their global body's involvement in Rhodesia, were determined to silence the one man anxious to tell the truth?

¶ 113 THE SILENCING OF PASTOR MUSA

The Rev. Arthur Lewis was not the only religious personality banned from our shores during the period of the Rhodesian U.D.I. The leader of the Apostolic Revival Movement, Pastor Ndabezinhie Musa, also had his concessionary passport withdrawn. A letter from the Foreign and Commonwealth Office dated 29 September 1978, and reproduced on an adjoining page, indicates that Musa's association with the Rhodesia Christian Group had given him a political connotation, — which rather begs the question, since the founders of

Foreign and Commonwealth Office
London SW1A 2AH

Telephone 01- 233 8727

Rev Fr A R Lewis
PO Box MP 177
Mount Pleasant
Salisbury
RHODESIA

Your reference

Our reference CP 043/1

Date 3 January 1979

Dear Father Lewis,

Thank you for your letter of 1 December to Miss Walkington who has now left this Department.

I regret to have to inform you that you have been made subject to travel and passport restrictions under the terms of Mr George Thomson's statement to Parliament of 27 June 1968 (copy enclosed) as a person "whom the Secretary of State has reason to believe to have furthered or encouraged .... the unlawful actions of the illegal regime". The Advisory Committee on Rhodesian Travel Restrictions recommended that this action should be taken because of your frequent expressions of sympathy and support for the regime, both written and oral.

You may submit an appeal against this decision to the Advisory Committee at any time. Written appeals should be addressed to Rhodesia Department, Foreign and Commonwealth Office, for onward transmission to the Committee; any requests for legal representation should also be sent to this Department in the first instance.

Yours sincerely,

R.W. Barnett

R W Barnett
Rhodesia Department

The banning of Father Lewis

the RCG would claim that it had only come into existence to resist the increasing politicisation of the established churches under the influence of the WCC.

So who was making politics out of what? And why did the Commonwealth Office ban Pastor Musa? Unlike Arthur Lewis, he could scarcely be said to have identified himself with "the illegal regime". In fact for the first few years of the Rhodesian U.D.I. he was actively involved as a "freedom fighter", intent on driving the white man out of Africa. His conversion to Christianity was reported to have been sudden and overwhelming, and the essence of his subsequent apostolic teaching was a reconciliation of racial differences within the framework of the Christian faith. Despite an earlier flirtation with Marxism, Musa was no compromiser of the eternal values. He identified the humanists in the church as pseudo-Christians, and criticised the manner in which they contrived to create differences of class and colour.

A devout soul and a sturdy one, Pastor N.B. Musa! Not much in a physical sense, but spiritually possessed of a lion-like courage and resolution. When the author met him he was moving in and out of the war zone in pursuit of his mission, daily courting death at the hands of some trigger-happy guerrilla armed with a sophisticated Russian rifle.

He would have had a stirring and an uplifting message for those British congregations who wanted to hear him. A black man! A true man of the people! Living amongst them and sharing their hopes and fears! What a harbinger of peace and conciliation he might have been at that critical stage in the war! Should the Foreign Office not have been delighted to have him over, to interview him, let him talk, put forth his point of view? After all, they had already fallen over themselves to grant passports and special favours to many a loud-mouthed desperado who had chosen the path of violent revolution.

Musa preached peace and conciliation. So *he* was banned. Is there not a moral there somewhere? Arthur Lewis had hinted darkly at the influence which the new generation of politicised churchmen seemed able to exert upon government policy in the United Kingdom. In this case also was it the clerical, rather than the temporal power, which could not stand up to criticism?

CHAPTER XIV

¶ 114 THE POLITICS OF TERROR

Terror! The technique of indiscriminate slaughter whereby populations are conditioned by grief, fear and hopelessness into accepting a revolutionary takeover! The Chinese attempted it unsuccessfully in Malaya. Aided by American subversives, Ho Chi Minh used it with telling effect during the Vietnam War. Following the conquest of Cuba, and Fidel Castro's compact with Moscow for the export of revolution, the legendary Che Guevara was sent to test its social disruptiveness on various South American republics. It was still going on, — aimlessly and apparently endlessly, — in the six counties of Northern Ireland, where a divided Catholic Church alternately blessed and reviled the killers and bombers, and where religious bigotries allowed the Marxist-inspired I.R.A. to conceal their revolutionary aims under a cloak of sectarian violence.

But the terror tactics of killing, maiming, burning and torturing took on a new dimension when practised in the context of Southern Africa. The savage heart of the Bantu had not been tamed in less than a century of contact with Western culture. There were natural cruelties in the tribal customs which, shocking and offensive as they might be to the civilised European, were acceptable to the African as a norm, — and which, under the conditions of guerrilla war, could be varied and adapted to produce nigh-unimaginable atrocities.

Hearts were cut out. Stomachs were ripped open. Young women had their vaginas seared with redhot irons. With the men it was not uncommon to find that their genitals had been cut off and stuffed into their mouths before shooting or stabbing and burning with petrol. And in a throwback to old cannibalistic practices, a black Rhodesian Christian in the Mount Darwin area had his ears, lips, and fleshy parts of the nose and chin cut off by visiting guerrillas, who then forced the man's wife to roast the flesh on an open fire and eat it under their supervision.

¶ 115 MASSACRE AT THE MUSAMI MISSION

Even more degrading assaults on human dignity had taken place during a mass raid on Portuguese settlements in Northern Angola. This was coordinated and timed with military precision along a four hundred mile front, concentrating upon isolated villages, farms and plantations where a few European families lived with their African house staffs and community workers. All who came within reach of the raiders' clubs, knives and machetes were promptly struck down, disembowelled, castrated or hideously disfigured. The women, both black and white, were stripped and repetitively raped before being hacked to pieces. Young children were taken from their cots and shorn of their arms and legs before being kicked around in a macabre game of football. As an added refinement, one group of terrorists, stumbling upon some woodworking machinery, switched on the circular saw and sliced up their victims lengthwise.

That had happened as far back as March 1963. Nothing that was still to happen in Rhodesia could be expected to outmatch it for scale or sheer primeval bestiality. But between the Z.A.N.U. and Z.A.P.U. wings of the guerrilla forces, concentrated in their respective tribal strongholds of Mashonaland and Matabeleland, and finding shelter and refuge in the neighbouring states of Mozambique and Botswana, there was a certain element of morbid competition in the grisly business of winning over the native populations through death, famine and disease.

To that end some of the guerrilla forays appeared to operate on a certain grim logic, as when they systematically prevented the tribesmen from dipping and inoculating their cattle against tropical infections, and murdered all the agricultural inspectors and supervisors who were unfortunate enough to fall into their hands. At other times the killings, maimings and atrocities would take place without rhyme or reason, — or perhaps in retribution for some slight or insult which an individual terrorist leader had taken to heart, as when a bold Casanova operating in 1977 on the Mozambique border, having failed to win the favours of a kraal headman's daughter, staked her out between two trees, soaked her in kerosene and burned her alive.

Erratic or systematic however, whimsical or planned, the scattered and unpredictable atrocities which seared the once peaceful Rhodesian countryside *were all rated as credits in the terror war* by the guerrilla commanders and their WCC sponsors until the massacre at St. Paul's Mission, Musami in February of 1977. At about ten o'clock on a Sunday evening three Roman Catholic missioner priests and four nuns were taken from their quarters and gunned down by a group of armed men who surprised them out of the darkness, and despatched them with the very minimum of ceremony. Father Dunstan Myerscough, an eighth member of the mission staff, was himself lined up for execution along with the others, but escaped death by falling amongst the falling bodies of his companions, and played possum until the killers had run away. It was his factual account of the massacre which was reported in the world press during the following few days. The executioners were all Africans, and he had assumed, as did the official recorders and the news reporters, that the attack had been carried out by Z.A.N.U. guerrillas armed and sent across the Mozambique border by Robert Mugabe.

But there was to be a dramatic twist to this all-too-familiar tale of apparently pointless bloodletting. For one thing, the sole surviving Catholic father had claimed that he and his colleagues regarded themselves as immune from terrorism, since they identified completely with the children and community helpers on their mission, and were dedicated only to their instruction and welfare. Also, Robert Mugabe himself was reputed to be "a sincere Roman Catholic" who would normally respect the sanctity of denominational missions working for the good of the indigenous African, and there was alarm in some quarters that the whole terrorist campaign might be getting out of control.

¶ 116 BLAMING THE SELOUS SCOUTS

At that point rumours started circulating about an under-cover branch of the Rhodesian Security Forces called the Selous Scouts, which was known to operate extensively in enemy territory, and might not be beyond setting up some nasty incidents for which the terrorists would get the blame. Sensing the implications, and taking his cue when it was offered, Mugabe himself issued an announcement to the international press that it was regular Rhodesian troops who had done the Musami killings. Subsequently an American mission sister, after three months in the country, would depart from Salisbury under duress, proclaiming that *all* atrocities were committed by the Rhodesian armed forces. And the local correspondent of a London Sunday newspaper reported some Catholic priests had assured him their black congregations were convinced it was Selous Scouts who were killing missionaries.

All this was valuable material for those churchmen on the WCC Central Committee who had voted funds for Mugabe's Z.A.N.U. guerrillas, and whose ideological commitment might still rebound upon them if the latter were seen to be slaying indiscriminately. In July of 1977, five months after the Musami massacre, *One World,* the aptly named magazine of the World Council of Churches, published an exclusive feature entitled "Who really kills civilians in Rhodesia?" Reproduced on an adjacent page, this article quotes extensively from unnamed Rhodesian army deserters whose country of refuge had evidently been heavily censored before it went to print. When questioned, those former soldiers were quite willing to agree that it was the Scouts who killed the Christian missionaries. "*. . . in the last ten years this war has been going on, there have been no missionaries or anyone like that shot. It is all of a sudden now. The Smith Government knows that the guerrillas are getting money from the churches so they strike at the missions so people will go against the guerrillas.*"

That, O fellow Christian, is the allegation that the official WCC magazine saw fit to publicise in its issue of July/August 1977, — using statements which had been prompted from disaffected personnel whom it could not name, and whose whereabouts could not be given. The inference was that missionaries had been a protected species during the earlier stages of the guerrilla war, and that this state of affairs had only altered after the World Council started paying money to Z.A.N.U. and Z.A.P.U. In a fit of pique the Rhodesian Government had supposedly then instructed one of its specialised commando units to avenge itself on the missions.

One World exclusive:

Who really kills civilians in Rhodesia?

Who really is responsible for the murder of civilians in war-torn Rhodesia? At least part of the answer seems to lie with the Selous Scouts, an elite commando-style unit of the Rhodesian Army itself.

Sinister rumours about the counter-insurgency role of the Scouts have been filtering out of Rhodesia for months. The British press has carried several reports on the Scouts, most notably from *Observer* correspondent David Martin who on March 13 quoted several Catholic priests in Rhodesia as saying that their African congregations were convinced the killings of missionaries were being carried out by Selous Scouts.

After a series of exhaustive interviews with Rhodesian Army deserters now living in [redacted], World Council of Churches staff writers have pieced together a clearer picture of the Selous Scout operation. The implications of this new information are enormous for church bodies helping to shape international understanding of the Rhodesian war. And the World Council of Churches itself, having given non-military aid to all three of the liberation movements working on the borders of and within Rhodesia, has a special interest in discovering the true nature of the conflict. Because all the blame for civilian killings to date has been levelled at the freedom fighters.

According to the deserters' testimonies, the Selous Scouts is a special army unit largely manned by black soldiers who dress, arm and operate exactly as guerrilla units of the liberation movements, even to the point of the few white soldiers involved disguising themselves as blacks. The white soldiers, who usually command these units, have been identified as originating not only from Rhodesia but also from Britain, Australia, USA, Germany, France and in larger numbers from South Africa.

Passing themselves off as guerrillas, the Scouts enter villages in the war zone to gather information and test the villagers' loyalty to the Smith Government. Where complicity with real freedom fighters is suspected, the Scouts act by killing villagers, or when hundreds are involved, by arranging for their imprisonment in "containment camps".

The Scouts' strategies vary but a favoured approach was described by one informant who had been in active service with a unit that supported Scout operations: "This big village is supporting guerrillas so they push Scouts in first. They go in and speak to the headman, get food and information, then move out. About 45 minutes later you get a load of army guys moving in following the tracks of these Scouts. They know that the Scouts were in there so they go to the headman and say, 'We're looking for a crew of guerrillas and we have traced them here.'

"The headman will say, 'I don't know anything about it.' And the soldiers say, 'But they were here, there are tracks coming in.' The headman still won't give information so the troops leave and contact the Scouts who return to the village and say, 'You have told the army where we are.' Then they wipe the village out. Other villagers hear the story and don't know what to think. It becomes impossible to define who are Scouts and who are guerrillas."

Evidence for the Scouts' actions is largely circumstantial because they operate in strict seclusion, even from other army units. "When Scouts are in an area, everything is frozen," said one deserter. "All the troops are either moved out beforehand, or you are kept stationary and not allowed to move from your position."

Once the Scouts have finished their work and withdrawn, troops move in. What they find varies from operation to operation. In some cases, intelligence units proceed the troops by helicopter. "They go and dig a couple of holes and throw the bodies in, throw some gasoline on and burn them, then cover them up. That is the normal practice," we were told.

Usually the troops find survivors who are left to share the belief that their village was attacked by real liberation fighters. "When the Scouts make a kill they always leave someone alone to tell the story. If guerrillas kill they kill everyone, but Selous Scouts are different. They massacre and then they leave someone to tell the story."

The deserter who told us this had himself visited a village two days after it had been "frozen" and entered by a Scout unit. Bodies of villagers they killed had been removed, but [redacted] African men and a woman were left to tell the story.

The massacre they described allegedly took place in a small village. Where larger populations are under suspicion, they are herded into containment camps, fenced in by diamond mesh and barbed wire fences and guarded at night by a cordon of searchlights. Anyone who moves outside the camp, once the lights are on, is shot. Conditions inside these camps are reported to be appalling. Medical care is sporadic, hygiene standards break down and disease is prevalent.

Just how many of the civilian murders in Rhodesia can be attributed to Selous Scout operations is impossible to say. Were Scouts involved, for example, in the much-publicized recent killings of Christian missionaries?

In reply to that question one ex-soldier we talked to pointed out that "in the last ten years this war has been going on, there have been no missionaries or anyone like that shot. It is all of a sudden now. The Smith Government knows that the guerrillas are getting money from the churches so they strike at the missions so people will go against the guerrillas."

The men we talked to offered that as a possibility. What they were certain of was the reputation of the Selous Scouts for ruthlessness, their claim to have the highest "kill rate" of any army unit, and the Scouts' open boast that they operate at will across the Mozambique border.

The prestige these Scouts enjoy within the Rhodesian Army is enormous. It contrasts sharply with the reputation of the Coloured troops whose morale from all accounts is at an all-time low. ("Coloured" denotes people of mixed racial origin whose political rights are limited and defined separately from Black Rhodesians.) We heard stories of Coloured soldiers going on strike for pay equal to European troops, complaining that their limited training made them easy targets in action, and that their lack of political rights in Rhodesia made it not worth fighting anyway.

But the dissatisfaction of Coloured troops isn't the army's only problem. Administration is lax in many areas, we were told. Leave and discharge papers are easily and often stolen. Lawlessness by troops increasingly goes unpunished. Rape cases are common. "I have seen soldiers shoot villagers," said one deserter. "But when a lawyer tried to take legal action, they tore up his papers and said you can't take the army to court. What the army does is in the interests of the country, so what they do is right."

It is exactly that sort of reasoning that makes the true role of the Selous Scouts so hard to dig out. And until the full story is told, the Scouts' record remains ugly and ominous.

What other incidents were taking place round about that time? Well, in December of 1976 Bishop Adolf Schmitt of Lupane, accompanied by two nuns and a priest, was motoring along a lonely dirt road in Matabeleland en route to visit a sick friend. They were stopped by a lone African gunman who held them up and demanded money. When they revealed that they were missionaries, and had no money with them, he gunned down the bishop, the priest and one of the nuns. The other, Sister Ermenfried Knauer, escaped with leg injuries when she dived beneath the car. She reported afterwards that before the shooting started, the killer had declared that "missionaries are enemies of the people".

Bishop Schmitt was one of those clerics who openly claimed immunity on account of his selfless devotion to black Africans. Yet he had been shot down by a loner who regarded him as an enemy of the people. Was this also the work of the Selous Scouts? And had Sister Knauer's testimony been falsified?

During the remainder of 1977 two other Roman Catholic priests were found to have been murdered, and their mutilated remains left in the bush. They were listed as Father Jose Manuel Rubio Diaz, a Spaniard, and Swiss-born Father George Joerger. Neither of these isolated incidents could possibly have been presented as propaganda killings, so it seemed that, despite the suspicions of *One World* magazine and its anonymous contributors, there were indeed terrorists with both the will and the motive for wiping out Christian missionaries.

From February of 1977 till the middle of 1978 there were no further massacres of mission staff in Rhodesia. Depending on your point of view, either the Selous Scouts had gone to ground, or Mugabe had managed to persuade his raiding parties that they were embarrassing the WCC. Then in June of 1978 there was a series of incidents right across Mashonaland, the most horrific of which being an attack upon a mission run by the Pentecostal Church in the Vumba Mountains near Umtali. Eight British missionaries and four children, including an infant, were brutally slain, their bodies sprawled in a grotesque heap on the grass outside their compound.

The Massacre at the Pentecostal Mission, Umtali

(Reproduced from "The Mind Benders")

¶ 117 WHY MARXIST GUERRILLAS KILLED CHRISTIAN MISSIONARIES

Once again Robert Mugabe promptly blamed the atrocity upon the Rhodesian Security Forces. But this time he had no hope of evading responsibility, for the raiders were known to have crossed the Mozambique border, and had identified themselves by speaking to some black school children. This time also there was no attempted cover-up by the *One World* magazine. The Z.A.N.U. gang had wiped out an entire mission complement of men, women and children, all white, and all dedicated, as with their counterparts at Lupane and Musami, to the welfare and education of the indigenous African.

Why? why? why? when it was so counter-productive to their cause? so potentially explosive for their patrons and paymasters of the WCC Central Committee? Were those guerrillas completely out of control once loaded up with supplies and ammunition, and sent out on their depredations? Did they kill by whim or reflex action? And had they not learned to differentiate between the enemy, be he civil or military, and those neutralist elements who could never be a danger to them?

One answer to this lay in the training and indoctrination which the guerrillas received before they were allowed to go on operations. Their instructors were exclusively Marxist, and it was in accordance with the Marxist philosophy of revolution by violent change that they ventured forth to impose their reign of terror. One festering suspicion which had been thrust to the forefront of their minds concerned the mission schools, and the influence which they continued to have on African primary education. This factor had already been impressed upon the Matabele guerrilla leader Josh N'komo by his Cuban advisers, hence the burning of schools and the abduction of school children into Botswana by Z.A.P.U. in 1977.

Mugabe's men were meanwhile being told by their political commissars that there would be no room for mission schools or any other type of private education in the new Zimbabwe, that all educational, cultural and economic activities must be controlled by the state. So it made sense to "take out" those Pentecostalists who, by their basic Christian teaching, would make it just that much harder

The Beast was getting his claws out through the clerical clothing

to convert their black pupils to the revolutionary philosophy of Karl Marx.

Now! anyone seriously believe that the Musami and Umtali massacres were master-minded and carried out by blue-eyed Rhodesian boys who had blackened their faces and taken on the demeanour and bestial instincts of the guerrilla enemy just to add one more horrifying statistic to the lengthening catalogue of terror?

¶ 118 WHO CARES WHAT HAPPENS IN FAR-OFF PLACES?

We have come a long way, haven't we, as we endeavour to pinpoint the motives and plumb the depths of depravity to which those global ecclesiasts at the WCC will reduce themselves as they strive for a one-world collectivist government administered by an all-conforming universal church? For some time now the Beast has been pushing his head and his fangs out through the clerical clothing, — or haven't you noticed?

You should not really have been surprised that the staff reporters at *One World* magazine seized upon the flimsiest of evidence in an attempt to protect their client guerrilla factions and blacken the reputation of the Rhodesian Security Forces. After all, when you take to working for the humanists, you are guided in your moral standards by *situation ethics,* which, as we have already seen, is just a synonym for the good old Leninist precept that the end always justifies the means.

All right, of course, whilst it was happening six thousand miles away in Southern Africa! From time to time the thought arises that this nauseating tale of ecclesiastically sponsored slaughter, bestiality and bearing of false witness, might just be a big yawn to the ordinary denizen of Mitcham, Manchester or Muddlecombe-cum-Tooting, who had always felt that those who went missionarising in exotic places just had to take their chances, and that black folks were natural savages who didn't need WCC encouragement to chop each other to pieces. Like other well-fed, inherently stable and tolerantly based societies, the British have generally adopted an other-worldly approach to what goes on in far off foreign parts, treating those distant cataclysms and disasters as something which has absolutely no relevance to their own civilised, well-ordered lives.

As for that 1968 decision by the Central Committee of the World Council of Churches to initiate a programme against racism,— well, it had to come, hadn't it? Those white supremacists in places like Angola, Mozambique, Rhodesia and South Africa were simply exploiting and discriminating against the blacks, denying them civil rights and equal opportunity in their own countries, so why should anyone in the caring, sharing Western World bother very much *how* the situation was rectified, — whether by sustained civil insurgency, clerical skulduggery or patient KGB manipulation?

Programme to Combat Racism! *Sure, I'll donate my foreign missions contribution to that humane and righteous cause, if it means that somewhere a little black youngster will grow up to lead a better, fuller life.* Even if it means that this particular youngster didn't grow up at all, since the money I put in the collecting plate was used to buy supplies and propaganda support for the bunch of marauders who rounded up his family and burned them to death in the kraalman's hut!

¶ 119 BUT NOW IT'S HAPPENING IN BRITAIN

Friend! Brother! Comrade! There's something you really ought to know. The clerical architects of the WCC Programme to Combat Racism did not stop at funding and propagandising for wars of racial emancipation in Darkest Africa. Among other things, they devoted considerable money and energy to the combatting of racism within these British islands. The British, according to WCC spokesman Dr. Phillip Potter, are one of the most racist peoples in history, so when Black Power arrived here in 1965 in the shape of the notorious Malcolm X, there were any number of frock-coated scarecrows ready to greet him as a new Messiah.

The advocates and adherents of Black Power latterly became known as the Black Muslims, after their spiritual leader Fard Muhammad persuaded them that they could only aspire to freedom, justice and equality under the standard of Islam because the Cross of Christ was a sign of death rather than of life, and because the white people who worshipped Christ had planned for the black man's destruction. Despite this unpropitious exhortation towards future racial harmony, — and the clear commitment to a militant faith which in times past had acted as a persecutor of Christians and Christianity, — the home-based British Council of Churches hastened to enter into consultation with the new movement, and it was as a result of this association in 1969 that the Programme to Combat Racism was launched a year later.

When the grants started to roll off in 1970, a coloured immigrant group in Britain was an immediate beneficiary. As noted by Bernard Smith in "The Fraudulent Gospel", this organisation, the West Indian Standing Conference, had been formed legitimately enough to assist with the settlement problems of an ethnic minority newly domiciled in an unfamiliar environment. But long before the World Council of Churches cast an approving eye over its shoulder and contributed to its funding, the W.I.S.C. had turned aside from its initial policy of friendly integration, and concentrated instead upon the politics of Black Power and racial confrontation. That the WCC anti-racist programmers were well aware of this, was conveyed by the terms of the grant, which was apparently awarded "to promote solidarity among the black community" and create "a strong grass roots *black power base"* which, in the stated opinion of the donors, might best protect them from the racist British society in which they found themselves.

How now, O indigenous citizen of Birmingham, Bermondsey and Bexley Heath? It's no longer the white racial supremacist of Bulawayo or Bloemfontein who's being hammered. The global ecclesiasts of the WCC have looked down on you from on high, and judging your latent repressiveness *in camera,* have ruled that there is also a liberation struggle to be waged in Smethwick, Southall and Kensington South.

Their first grant for the alleviation of alleged white racism in Britain was set at £3,500. There was a similar allocation some three years later to the Institute of Race Relations, another initially non-partisan, non-political body which had started out with the laudable intent of integrating coloured minorities into indigenous society, but ended up as an instrument of Black Power. The new revolutionary grouping which formed out of the discredited and emasculated Institute was called T.R.J. (Towards Racial Justice), it was undeniably disruptive in character and Marxist in composition, —and the WCC promptly rewarded it with a further grant of £4,500. By April of 1981, — the month of the Brixton riots, — it was claimed that T.R.J. and its magazine *Race Today* had received a total of £60,000 from British and global ecclesiastical funds.

¶ 120 TOWARDS RACIAL HATRED

Now if you imagine at this stage that the money must have been wheedled out of our clerical innocents by some sort of smooth-talking confidence trickster able to put an idealistic interpretation upon his struggle for the rights of coloured people, you are due to be immediately disillusioned. For the acknowledged leader of T.R.J. is Darcus Howe, a Marxist orator from Trinidad who pulls no punches, and makes no secret of his appetite for a perpetual state of racial confrontation, in which the blacks would manifest their "revolutionary potential for the development of the working class as a whole", and become "one of the most potent forces of revolutionary change in Britain".

Mr. Howe exulted that the Brixton riots had illustrated how young West Indians were able to fight back against police harassment by sticks and bricks and petrol bombs. And as noted in the "Sunday Express" of 26th April 1981, he also exuded a spirit of jovial camaraderie for all other violent, militant and essentially revolutionary activists who from time to time jeopardised the Queen's peace. From a public platform he took it upon himself to pledge the full support of the black community for the I.R.A. gunmen and bombers who were trying to sicken the British Government out of its commitment to the majority view in Northern Ireland, and for good measure he added a flippant, callous and utterly tasteless verdict upon the booby trap murder of Mr. Airey Neave, M.P., known for his firm line on the Irish troubles.

Mr. Neave was also a much decorated hero of the Second World War, and a broadly respected member of the Christian society which had brought that war to a victorious conclusion, ensuring democratic freedom of thought and action to millions who would use those gracious gifts more justly and legitimately than Mr. Darcus Howe.

Yet it was Darcus Howe and his scurrilous, abusive and racially bigoted magazine which kept getting repeated injections of WCC money.

¶ 121 COMPROMISING CHRISTIAN ETHICS

That's it, fellow Christian! fellow countryman! fellow subscriber to the belief that preservation of our broadly tolerant Western society is the best hope for all humanity, whatever its colours or its creeds. We've taken a searching look at the globalist church organisation which has assumed ideological and administrative responsibilities for all of Christendom, — and none of us can be very happy with what we see.

It does not really matter what you think about social and economic inequalities, ethnic differences, the rights of former colonial peoples to practise self-determination even at the risk of their own impoverishment and eventual subjugation by power cliques of their own kind. The Church is always entitled to take an independent view of such matters, and to pursue its holy mission without fear or favour. What it has never any right to do is to compromise Christian ethics in a dialogue with Marxist materialism. This we have observed it to do many times in the chapters that are behind us, and we must surely be agreed upon the depths to which it has sunk in its efforts to find a lowest common denominator as between the eternal biblical truths and the tortuous ideological posturings of secular humanism.

Father Arthur Lewis quotes the eminent Professor Julian Huxley, first director-general of UNESCO, as having argued that Christian ethics, Christian values and principles, once so thoroughly rooted, would survive quite independently of Christian belief. The tale of horror and unimaginable atrocity which Lewis had to tell in "Christian Terror" was an utterly devastating indictment of the flaws in Huxley's reasoning.

Of course Huxley's fellow humanists have known this for a long time. They may privately regret that their materialistic creed has been unable to capitalise upon the ethics and upstanding values of a Christian past. They will certainly bluster and obfuscate to avoid exposure of their own positions, — but with every twist and wriggle they will only find themselves more deeply enmeshed in a web of intrigue, false witness and double-standard morality.

CHAPTER XV

¶ 122 NO SOLUTION IN NORTHERN IRELAND?

Depending upon your point of view, what do you think of the never-ending Irish troubles? The bombings, maimings and killings! The persistent shooting down of off-duty policemen, sometimes in their own homes, often in front of their families! The occasional assassination of some celebrity who has dared to speak out in condemnation of the violence! The booby-trapping of commercial properties and motor vehicles, with the inevitable spillage of innocent blood! The calamitous destruction of buildings and frequent disruptions of social and economic life! The funeral processions! The tear-stained faces of women and children who have lost their husbands and their fathers! The stock phrases and solemn expressions of television newsreaders as they announce the daily toll in human life and the extension of private misery! The prevailing consensus of press and broadcast media alike that it is all pre-destined and inevitable, an insoluble problem that will not alleviate or go away!

Is that what *you* think, — that barring a surrender to the I.R.A., or a casting adrift of the whole of Erin's isle, there's nothing to be done but stoically endure the bombings, shootings, hunger strikes and various other forms of psychological warfare, till some hitherto unimagined initiative emerges which will satiate the sectarian factions and pension off the gunmen and the bombers?

Her Majesty's Government, the Ulster constabulary, superbly

trained commando and special service units of the British army upstaged, outmanoeuvred and fought to a standstill by a bunch of hooded hoodlums financed by Irish American dollars, and sheltered within the bosom of a Catholic community which has lost all faith in law and justice! Nobody puts it quite so bluntly, but nevertheless the inference is there, — that the law, the police and the military have grievously failed to protect life and limb, and to restore the Queen's peace in an integral part of her shrinking dominion.

Can we believe it? Must we accept it? That the Anglo-Saxon race which has dared and improvised itself out of every disaster from the Spanish Armada to the beaches of Dunkirk, should suddenly have lost all its resolve, moral fibre, ingenuity and sheer cussed determination to win through regardless? If it be so, *then what on earth has changed?*

¶ 123 DEFENCELESS AGAINST THE KILLERS

Following the murder of the Reverend Robert Bradford, M.P. by I.R.A. gunmen in November of 1981, there was a totally understandable reaction from an Ulster Protestant community which felt more than ever that its hearths and homes had been wantonly exposed to the assassin's gun. But when another Ulster clergyman, the burly Ian Paisley, M.P., tried to harness the popular indignation by forming his own supporters into an armed militia, the authorities and the media submitted him to more abuse and criticism than they had managed to conjure up against the killers.

Why? In such a situation, when an entire population fears that its most active and most public-spirited members have become human targets for a band of roving paranoiacs armed with sophisticated weaponry, surely the official riposte should be a range of energetic and wide-reaching security measures designed to stop the slaughter at all costs, and restore public confidence. Paisley's call to arms was triggered by a pessimistic realisation that what various governments had failed to do in twelve years of urban guerrilla strife was unlikely to happen then.

He was right, wasn't he? The Irish Secretary, James Prior, sonorously deplored the latest atrocities and affirmed his Government's resolve to pursue the killers until they were brought to justice. More crack troops were sent across the Irish Sea to join their mates in the operational area. There was a surge in security forces activity, and a promise that specialist undercover tactics would be made more effective. It might have sounded adequate and reassuring to an interested bystander in far-off Honolulu, but it did nothing for an Ulsterman who knew that there might be a hit-squad in his front porch next time he answered the door, or a gun pointed at his back if he walked in a darkened street. The game was still being played according to a set of rules which had been fixed above the heads of the players, and there was only one result which would bring on the final whistle.

¶ 124 PRESS AND TV SUPPORT FOR THE I.R.A.

It needed a change of tactics and emphasis, didn't it? The institution of a *search and interrogate* procedure that paid more heed to the circumstances of the emergency than to the European Court of Human Rights! An immediate, if temporary, clampdown of movements across the Eirann border, — ruinous and difficult as that might prove to be! Some registration and restriction on Southern Irish citizens travelling in Ulster and other parts of the United Kingdom! The certainty of a death sentence on anyone found guilty of a terrorist killing anywhere within the jurisdiction of H.M. Government!

Yes, restoration of the death penalty! Society degenerating into motives of revenge! Re-institution of judicial murder! Call it what you will. The principal objective of such and other possible measures would be to stop the killings; and that, in the author's understanding, is a first prerogative of responsible government.

So why is everything made to seem so diabolically complicated these days? Why are police and other security organisations so inhibited from pursuing their main task of protecting life and property? Why especially do we find in such an atrocious and bloody business as the Irish shootings and bombings, that there is a popular press and a strong television lobby which in content and sentiment reacts more sympathetically to the doings of the Provisional I.R.A. than to the legitimate forces of law and order?

Simplistically one might respond that in any sectarian struggle even the itinerant journalist or Tv producer reacts according to his origins, so that wherever the media had a fair representation of Irish Catholics, there one might find instinctive support for the United Ireland cause.

¶ 125 ENTER THE KGB

Yet the Protestant-Catholic confrontation in Northern Ireland has long ago ceased to be a struggle for unification or civil rights, and become instead a proving ground for Marxist revolution. In "The Terror Network" Claire Sterling, an American foreign correspondent, describes how the I.R.A. made contact with the Palestine Liberation Organisation as far back as 1969, and sent some of its members to train in Jordanian guerrilla camps. Thenceforth it was represented at the councils of a worldwide terrorist network which was to encompass the Red Brigades of Italy and Japan, Germany's Baader-Meinhof, the South American Tupamaros, the Basque ETA resistance movement and Libyan hit-squads financed and controlled by President Gaddafi.

The facts are no longer in contention. When the Marxist intellectual Antonio Negri was arrested in 1979 on charges which established him as a veritable godfather to Italy's Red terrorist revolution, the ensuing court proceedings not only uncovered active subversion and complicity at every level of Italian society, but also a "close and permanent contact" with the Baader-Meinhof in Germany, the Basque ETA terrorists in Spain, the Palestine Liberation Front in the Middle East and the I.R.A. in Ireland.

Claire Sterling further relates how in the early years of the "troubles", the Provisionals' search for sophisticated weaponry took them to an arms factory in Czecho-Slovakia run by the Czech security service and controlled by the KGB. Here they were able to order bazookas, rocket-launchers, hand grenades, automatic rifles and stocks of ammunition. Subsequently the KGB set up a presence in Dublin, fair-seemingly to monitor the arms traffic, but also to give the benefit of its own unique experience in the business of terrorism and subversion. Vladimir Kozlov, sent to Eire under the guise of a Tass correspondent, had been identified in 1975 as a specialist in assassination and sabotage.

¶ 126 THE COMPLIANCE OF 'THE SECOND SOCIETY'

So! we have it on fairly good authority, backed up by a high court investigation, that the guerrilla war which had begun as a campaign for civil rights and a united Ireland, was now part of a closely-linked international terrorist network conspiring at the de-stabilisation and possible downfall of Western European democracy, — and as might well be expected, encouraged, resourced and strategically manipulated by the Russian KGB.

Does that give you any clues as to why the anti-terrorist campaign in Ulster always goes off at half-cock, and the security forces, police, army, commandos and all, are expected to hold themselves continually at risk whilst the fighting is conducted with one brawny military arm firmly screwed up behind a soldierly back? Does it help to explain the equivocal attitude of so many of our organs of mass-communication? Those cosy confidential interviews with I.R.A. killers following the most macabre and cold-blooded of atrocities! The Tv cameras which zero-ed in on the Belfast street riots that followed the deaths of the Maze hunger-strikers, — and which managed to make the throwing of missiles and Molotov cocktails into a television spectacular!

In this latter connection police and army riot control commanders would observe that the kids and the petrol bombers started following the camera crews, who were thereby prompted to inaugurate incidents of arson and police assault by offering the rioters the glamour of network television coverage. And in the latter half of May an Irish journalist related how, on the morning after the death of hunger-striker Raymond McCreesh, the B.B.C.'s radio announcement of a calm reaction on the streets of West Belfast was taken as a signal for the stoning, petrol bombing and lorry-burning to begin all over again.

It would appear that in such fragile situations the media goes beyond a mere reporting of the news, and takes a hand in its manufacture. And in the context of Northern Ireland, where so many organs of both press and radio have shown such a bias in favour of riot, arson and revolution, we have to ask ourselves who sends out those sensation-making reporters and camera crews, who gives them their instructions.

Remember the clearly established link between the Provisional I.R.A. and the international terror network. Remember the patronage, expertise and logistics support which it has enjoyed from the KGB. Programme in the illuminating disclosures made in Padua at the trial of the Italian revolutionary master-mind Professor Antonio Negri, — that many of Italy's socialist intellectuals had become the terrorists' unwitting accomplices, — and you have the conception of an amorphous social layer, outwardly respectable, reaching into the higher stratas of the commercial and professional establishment, yet readily susceptible to the methods and objectives of Marxist revolution. Carlo Fioroni, the former schoolteacher who turned state witness in the Negri trial, called them *the Second Society,* and there is no doubt that the demonic Paduan professor who came so near to destroying the Italian state with his murder gangs and concerted instruments of civil disruption and terror, valued the compliance and approval of his intellectual colleagues as much as he did his hit-men and the trade union moles who had brought the industrial north to a standstill.

¶ 127 AN ELITE WITH A VESTED INTEREST IN MURDER

Get the picture now? Does it begin to fit together? Revolution in the streets! Arson, bombing and intimidation! Assassination of prominent citizens, particularly those outspoken in their criticism of Marxist violence! Half-baked and insufficiently motivated efforts to contain the spread of lawlessness! A mysterious inertia on the part of the authorities when it comes to pinpointing the ideology which keeps the revolutionary bandwaggon rolling! And hovering patronisingly above it all, that *Second Society* of college dons, academics, professors of political science and sociology, left-wing journalists, producers and publicists; international speculators, promoters of shady and dubious enterprises, slick exponents of the good life, creaming it off at the top end of the social spectrum and apparently uncaring about what might happen if their nihilistic philosophy were carried to its logical conclusion!

Time to put a label on those elitists of the Second Society, isn't it? Time to give them a group identity and spot the common factor which keeps them pulling instinctively in the same direction! Fabians? Marxists? Intellectual agnostics? Humanists?

Aye, the humanists! Those prim and patronising do-gooders with their prayerful sermonisings on everything from human rights to the teacher's use of the tawse! Are you still finding it difficult to dispel this illusion of the humanist as a sane responsible, moderate-minded sort of chap who would never do anything without suitable reflection, and who would invariably choose the middle way if there was one? Not much moderation about international terror, is there? Or about the bombings and shootings in Northern Ireland?

The violent society did not simply happen. It was as much a product of long-range planning as the data-processing revolution or the computerised machine tool. And the humanists in this country are just as deeply implicated as were Professor Negri's socialist intellectuals when they connived at the diabolical outburst of shootings, kidnappings, industrial sabotage and Mafia-assisted criminality which brought Italy to the verge of anarchy.

CHAPTER XVI

¶ 128 HUMANIST PREFERENCES FOR THE AUTHORITARIAN STATE

It has been emphasised on a number of occasions that the ultimate goal of international humanism appears to be World Government, — a One World Super State ruled by some supra-national oligarchy which would seek to perpetuate itself in power just as the Politburo does in Soviet Russia. Whether indeed the Soviet collectivist system came to be the predominant force within that World Federation would depend upon how the Western Alliance manages to retain its capacity for manoeuvre against subversion, defeatism and outright military conquest. The humanists and their various internationalist collaborators would in any case favour some sort of authoritarian takeover, since their grand strategy is designed to be irreversible, and they would not propose to jeopardise their hard-won objectives at the whim of a democratic electorate.

Naturally there is resistance at all levels to the World Federalists' plan for global conformity, especially in so far as it involves a fusion of our Western way of life with the suppressed and fear-ridden societies of Eastern Europe. That fusion might be acceptable, — indeed desirable, — in circumstances where freedom and enlightenment were about to be extended to the deprived from the emancipated. But since the reverse is more likely to be the out-come, since any imminent surrender to the globalist concept would probably mean an extension of Communist bestiality all the way westwards to the Mountains of Connemara, and spreading south towards the Cape of Good Hope, the thoughtful majority have rightly decided that whatever its imperfections, our Western civilisation might just be worth preserving.

As a result the humanists and their kind have had to resort to a certain duplicity. They have tried to achieve by stealth that which they could never hope to gain by open persuasion, — and of course the manner of their progression has been a principal cause for the writing of this volume.

¶ 129 THE SECRET THAT DIED WITH JOHN F. KENNEDY

Earlier chapters have dealt with humanist penetration into the ecclesiastical sphere, but it stands to reason that if they are to advance their ambitions by the coercion and manipulation of governments, they must also make their influence felt in the political. Are there signs, therefore, of humanists or humanist sympathisers being propelled into positions of power where they might exert useful leverage in favour of humanist objectives?

We have instanced the impressive financial and political muscle that went into family planning, Planned Parenthood and World Population Control. The Sex Information and Educational Council of the United States was another private sectarian organisation which quickly acquired quasi-governmental status as it purported to guide the sexual development of future generations throughout the English-speaking world. We know that humanists have sat on high level advisory boards, in cabinets and privy councils and at the right hand of presidents. They have frustrated and confused social, economic and foreign policies till we are nigh unable to defend ourselves against a regressive ideology that could send us back to the Dark Ages. But to what extent have they made their mark on those supreme state offices which guide the destiny of nations?

A constant cause of concern to conservatives in the last twenty years has been the One Worlders' persistent endeavour to capture and manipulate the presidency of the United States. Several bizarre and sensational events in American history, such as Watergate and the shooting of John F. Kennedy, can be traced back to the power-mania of conspiratorial pressure groups intent on protecting or improving their own positions.

Kennedy, the golden boy of a heralded golden age, seemed to have achieved the supreme executive office in collaboration with the humanist-inspired Eastern Establishment, rather than in spite of them. So it might have been expected that whilst he conformed, his backing was assured, and the presidential chair would be his for as long as the constitution allowed him to stay. But John F. Kennedy was born of a devout Catholic mother, and though we are not privy to the particular aspect or aspects of humanist global policy which ultimately revolted him, we do know that in 1963, for some weeks prior to that fateful visit to Dallas, he had been wrestling with his Christian conscience, sometimes alone, sometimes in the presence of trusted confidants. It is reported that he finally decided to break with his influential backers, and had planned to make an announcement as soon as the Texas trip was over. Who knows? If the other facts are as stated, one of those trusted confidants must have had a loose tongue, or a bug in his vest pocket. Certainly the Kennedy assassination was followed by a disgraceful cover-up operation which should have convinced no one, and it was remarked a few years later that almost a score of people with intimate knowledge of that 1963 outrage had also lost their lives through suicide, murder or fatal accident. It looked as though the professional mafia who ran the hit campaign believed in the old dictum that dead men tell no tales.

¶ 130 THE DANGER TO AMERICAN SOVEREIGNTY

Jimmy Carter, who was elected to the oval office in November of 1976, described himself as a 'born-again Christian', and on that account was reckoned to have derived substantial support from the bible belt of the Mid South. But as reported in *The Lemming Folk,* his was not really the romance of a country boy making good. He had been secretly groomed and bankrolled by a shadowy Eastern Establishment which was for ever trying to pick its own winners, and then manipulate them for its own ends. Its reward in this case was to see prominent One Worlders installed in cabinet posts where their commitment towards *'a shared world and global measures'* would further weaken America's national resolve, and erode both the confidence and capability of her allies to resist Soviet penetration.

Carter the professing Christian also had a well-known humanist as his vice-president, and another as his secretary of state, whilst Andrew Young, his ambassador to the United Nations, gave lessons in Marxism to the emergent revolutionary factions of Southern Africa. Had the country boy from Plains in Georgia been able to persuade the American electorate to give him a second term, there is no knowing to what extent a self-confident humanist-orientated World Federalist oligarchy would have guided him into an irreversible sacrifice of American sovereignty.

¶ 131 PARA-PSYCHOLOGY AND THE OBSESSIVE KILLER

As things went, the Darwinist-humanist international seemed to have suffered a severe setback with the election of ex-film actor Ronald Reagan, who had come up the hard way as secretary of an actors' guild, and whose life experiences had confirmed him in his allegiance to an all-seeing God. So whatever pacts and compromises he had been obliged to make in his bid to become America's Premier Executive and virtual leader of the democratic nations of the Western hemisphere, *he was a man with a Christian conscience,* and as with John F. Kennedy, that could occasionally become embarrassing and inconvenient to the high-powered oligarchy which was planning to take the United States into a global federation, probably against its will.

What next? Well it just happened in the spring of 1981 that some confused young idiot was standing around with a lethal hand-gun when President Reagan was emerging from a routine lunchtime appointment in Washington, D.C. Shots were fired. One of the President's aides was severely injured, and he himself was hit more than once before the bodyguard shielded his person and smothered the assailant. Mercifully a much happier outcome than that tragic affair in Dallas! Ronald Reagan rode with the shots as he might have done in one of his former cowboy epics, and survived to fight another day. A lot of people would have cause to be grateful.

As for the would-be assassin, he came of a respectable and prosperous American family, and the only publicised pretext for his attempted outrage was a desire to project his longing for some starlet of the entertainment world. O.K. Just another isolated nutcase? In a pattern that was to be repeated some months later, when a paranoiac Armenian drew a bead on Pope John Paul II?

Come! come! After what we have learned about the International Terror Network, we should not be so simple. There is a very clear indication from informed sources that susceptible individuals can now be *programmed* to carry out specific acts of attrition and atrocity, — that it depends upon the skilful use of obsessive drugs, which are no longer confined to the realms of science fiction. It is claimed, for instance, that methadone, currently in clinical use to break heroin addicts from their affliction, can in itself become an instrument of mind control, weaning the pathetic victim from one area of obsession directly into another. The facts must be readily available to most espionage and intelligence agencies, including the Russian KGB, — so next time some revered national figure is gunned down by a confused youngster bemoaning the loss of his pocket money or the alienation of his girl friend, it might be relevant to look for the X factor which has its origins in the realm of para-psychological warfare.

¶ 132 THE FALLACY OF THE CENTURY

Right! We live in a terrible world, where the good and the righteous can be blasted down in front of our eyes, leaving our society just that much weaker, — where the miracles of science are often being used, not to benefit mankind, but to further the immoral aims of sinister pressure groups who dare not let us have advance knowledge of what they are planning to do.

Let's recognise it as a distinct possibility that once the Christian ethic has been thrust aside and discredited, there are powerful people who will stoop to *any* lengths to gain their objectives. Professor Julian Huxley had claimed that it need not be so, that Christian morality would survive independently of Christian belief, and the new humanist society would build upon the standards and the achievements of the old. This has proved to be the most horrendous fallacy of the twentieth century. For have we not had a frightening preview of the authoritarian crudities, the hedonistic perversities and the poisonous depravities into which our society will have descended if we ever allow the humanists to attain their global concept of a

World Super Government ministered by a World Super Church?

CHAPTER XVII

¶ 133 HUMANISTS AMONGST THE TORIES

The power shift which took place during the Second World War had left America as the financial and economic Colossus which dominated the politics and military strategies of the Western hemisphere. Therefore what happened in Washington or New York was taken to be of much more critical importance than similar events in London or Paris or Bonn. Getting at the White House or the Pentagon was reaching for the jugular vein, and none knew *that* better than the left-wing intelligentsia who were planning for a long-term re-alignment of our religious and social traditions.

Does this mean that what happens within these British islands no longer matters, that we can afford to go pacifist, humanist, unilateralist, effeminate, sloppy and drug-happy, — all without a thought to the consequences, — just because the big global decisions are likely to be taken a mile above our heads? Not a bit of it! There's a growing suspicion that in the One Worlder's notebook of snags, setbacks and intractable problems, *race* features just as prominently as supranational economics or numbers of nuclear missiles, — and that the one race which can for ever prove a stumbling block to a future One World tyranny is the bulldog breed which in the eighteenth and nineteenth centuries set out from these shores to spread its language and its culture to the four corners of the earth!

So it matters vitally what happens here in Britain, — in the churches and the factories, in the boardrooms and the exchanges, in the councils of the T.U.C. and the C.B.I. and the main political parties. The humanist-orientated internationalists are watching us closely, ready to take advantage of any trend or fashion which might tilt our destinies in their direction.

It was once felt that they had most to gain through a Fabian-dominated Labour movement linked to the socialist international, and infiltrated by all manner of subversives. That was why Harold Wilson enjoyed such a wonderful press during his earlier years in power, and why it took the British people such an incredibly long time to rumble his total lack of statesmanship. The nation survived in spite of him, and the party which he bequeathed to his successors was well on the way to fragmentation and a type of extremist dogmatism which would erode its political power base.

What of the Conservatives? Well, despite being the traditional party of God, Queen and Country, by the nineteen-seventies the Tories had gathered together their own motley assortment of supranational financiers, humanist-orientated reformers and World Government visionaries. Predictably therefore, when they got into power their policies disappointed no one more acutely than their own supporters. The trouble was that class and the old school tie could no longer be regarded as reliable barometers of conservatism. Even the KGB had started recruiting its agents on the ineffable superiority of their Oxbridge accents, — and it no longer required a confession of faith to be included in the Central Office list of approved parliamentary candidates.

Yet that was what was most urgently needed, — a confession of faith! Faith in one's country and its time-honoured institutions! Faith in one's own people, regardless of class or status or vocation! Faith in a Divine Being, and in the essentially Christian values which have given us the tolerant society which we know! By definition, humanists do not possess that faith, — and humanists in the Tory Party were busy nibbling away at the principles of Christian conservatism.

Aye, Christian conservatism! Does that sound like an anachronism to some people? And is it too much to ask that Christians and conservatives will start to think about it seriously? For the entire weight of our argument thus far is based upon the fact that you cannot have one without the other.

¶ 134 BIRTH OF THE S.D.P.

Thus with the old Labour Party losing the moral consciousness of its working-class origins, and the Tories suffering from a collapse of confidence as humanist ambiguities clouded their image, people began looking around for an alternative. And as so often happens, a seasoned performer was waiting in the wings.

Throughout the nineteen-sixties one of the great protagonists of Fabian-humanism was the former Labour Home Secretary and Chancellor Roy Jenkins, who had presided over the abolition of both capital and corporal punishment, and thereby done his little bit towards creation of the violent society. Roy retired from British politics during the seventies to take up an appointment with the European Commission, but some time in 1979, following Margaret Thatcher's arrival in Downing Street, he started looking back across the Channel and talking about a *radical centrist* alignment which would break up the two-party system.

Despite the years of voluntary exile amongst the fleshpots of Brussels, he is reputed to have maintained an intimate friendship with a certain Liberal politician who has already come to our notice in this volume. David Steel was an early supporter of humanist aims and ambitions when he sponsored the Abortion Bill through the House of Commons, and for this timely contribution to World Population Control had achieved a sort of special relationship with humanists in the media, who cultivated his public image so carefully that he received top popularity ratings from people who knew nothing about him or his obsession with One World internationalism.

When two prominent members of the British Fabian Society, Dr. David Owen and Mrs. Shirley Williams, defected from the Labour Party along with its Shadow Defence Minister William Rodgers, Roy Jenkins was back home waiting to receive them with open arms, and the Social Democratic Party was born, — not without accusations of plagiarism from a Right-wing Labour group called the Social Democratic Alliance, who had been fighting a sturdy battle for social democracy long before the members of the Gang of Four had even thought about it.

Jenkins and his colleagues brushed them aside as being of little consequence. Based upon their leader's cordial relations with David Steel, they had notions of another type of alliance, which eventually came to pass in the shape of a full electoral pact between Liberals and the newly formed S.D.P., under which they undertook to put up candidates alternately at by-elections, and to go into the next general election as a combined force intent on seizing political power.

¶ 135 THE WORLD FEDERALISTS GET TOGETHER

The by-election strategy was immediately successful. The Liberal no-hoper who had been retained to contest a constituency at Croydon in the autumn of 1981, now swept home to victory with the support of thousands who had decided that their future lay with the Social Democrats. Jenkins himself was tempted out on to the battlefield, and came close to defeating his old colleagues in what had formerly been a safe Labour seat. He would try again at the first opportunity. But meanwhile Mrs. Williams went to Crosby and overturned a previous 19,000 Conservative majority amid scenes of wild enthusiasm.

The British electorate had obviously had enough of confrontation politics as practised between the two major parties, and had given its blessing to the new alignment. As the Labour Party fell into disrepute with the moderate majority, more and more of its Right-wing M.P.s defected to the S.D.P. David Steel, apparently without any dissension among his Liberal colleagues, talked grandly about the Alliance forming the next government, and even threw out a lifeline to another world federalist, ex-Premier Ted Heath, who he thought might one day want to join them. Commenting upon Steel's vaulting ambitions in the aftermath of the Crosby by-election, the international magazine "Newsweek", which reflects the views of the One Worlders, suggested that Jenkins might groom him through one term of office before moving aside to bequeath him the leadership.

So there you are, folks. It had all happened within the short space of a few months, but already a long-headed humanist establishment was picking and promoting its own winners.

¶ 136 MERGING BRITAIN WITH THE SOVIET UNION

David Steel as a coming Prime Minister of Great Britain! You hadn't really thought seriously about that one, had you, —particularly whilst he was presiding over the rump of the Liberal Party? And if it came to pass as a result of the new political alignment, what kind of a prime minister would he be? In December of 1981, whilst discussing the possibility of working with the pseudo-conservative Ted Heath, he said that the latter's "views on domestic and economic policy and *the new international order"* were very close to Liberal views.

The new international order! Interesting to see him using those exact words! Do we have to spell out what they mean? The preceding sixteen chapters are a catalogue of the infiltrations, manoeuvrings, subversions, betrayals and revolutionary disruptions in which the humanists have from time to time involved themselves so that their *new international order* might one day come into being.

And how *could* it come into being? Only by a fusion of all the world's peoples into one great polyglot mass, where there would be a submersion of nationalities and ethnic differences and pride of race or heritage, — a destruction of all the cultures and traditions which make us what we are! As for the methods, some of its advocates have been disarmingly frank. Remember H. R. Gaither, that one-time president of the Ford Foundation, who admitted that his own purpose was "so to alter (American) society that it could be comfortably merged with that of the Soviet Union".

¶ 137 MEETING UP WITH THE ANTI-CHRIST

O.k! you find it difficult to believe that even a Liberal internationalist like David Steel would ever want to line up our British society for a merger with the Soviets in Moscow. Well maybe so! But One Worlders are always trying to advance their aims one way or another, and if a merger proved hopelessly impracticable, what about a takeover? In this age of chilling nuclear blackmail and strategic overkill, some things can happen very quickly, and it might be that under the stewardship of someone like Mr. Steel we only need to drop our guard for a year, or a month, or a day, — to find that we have foreign troops stationed in our kitchen, and blank looks of incomprehension when we ask them to go away.

In any case it should give us all serious thought that the projected new alignment in British politics had been master-minded by a

Fabian-humanist internationalist whose penal reforms whilst at the Home Office ushered in the violent society; that two of his founding members were also fellow Fabians, presumably with similar internationalist leanings; and that the lynch-pin of the Liberal/Social Democratic Alliance was a darling of the humanistic revolution, committed to some of the global objectives against which we have uttered the gravest of warnings in this volume.

It has surely been made very plain that whatever the religious views of its many tools, dupes and adherents, the humanist One World concept is not in itself a Christian inspiration. One might say in fact that it is the fair-seeming face of the Anti-Christ in our twentieth century *milieu.* Behind it lurks the Beast, with all his bestial impulses and brute insensitivities. As we have seen, we are no match for that beast unless we gird ourselves again with the faith that sustained our Christian forefathers.

¶ 138 WHY ORWELL DECIDED THERE WAS NO HOPE

In the nineteen-forties the former Communist visionary George Orwell was setting down his impressions of an internationalist-collectivist future in the novel "1984". Almost alone in its day, this book spelled out the ultimate consequences for all of us if Fabian-socialist One World policies were carried to their logical conclusion. Western society had good cause to be grateful for the warning, just as a traveller on a stormy night might breathe his heartfelt thanks to be advised that a chasm had opened in the dark and tortuous road that lay ahead. 1984 became the chasm in time against which our latter day philosophers would measure human progress, — either over and outwards into enlightenment, or headlong into the void.

Even so, for those who took Orwell seriously, who realised that so many of the collectivist horrors, so much of the social and human degradation that he envisaged could so easily come to pass, — that the show might already have had its dress rehearsal in the Stalinist era of Soviet Russia, — perhaps the most depressing thing was the final Orwellian conclusion that in a world dominated by such rigid authoritarian forces there could be *no hope.*

Why did the brilliant prophetically-gifted Orwell conclude that there was no hope? Remember that as a young man he had been brought up in the best traditions of Bloomsbury Fabianism, revering such father figures as Sidney Webb, G.B.S. and John Maynard Keynes, and looking towards the Marxist experiment in the U.S.S.R. as a kind of staging point to the Promised Land. He joined with thousands of other socialist idealists in the Spanish Civil War, and somewhere in the course of his military experiences or in the period of contemplation that followed, decided that the collectivist ideal to which he had devoted so many of his youthful years was really a monstrous evil. His scenario for "1984" was the triumph of that evil over all the enlightened and libertarian forces which had brought civilisation to its present level of advancement.

But coming as he did to abhor the impending conquest, he had failed, — through the atheistic agnosticism of his upbringing, — to diagnose *that one condition* which would have to be satisfied if Big Brother and his commissars were ever to feel secure in the Hell which they had created for their fellow mortals on Planet Earth.

Orwell could not think like a Christian. For him there were no hidden resources of the human soul. With the humanists he assumed that Man was in supreme command of his destiny, and that any resort to a Spiritual Being was utterly outmoded. He therefore tried to visualise the totalitarian monster of his One World Secretariat being challenged only by an alternative philosophy based on humanistic values, and concluded that in the face of such massive material and psychological superiority no successful challenge was possible.

¶ 139 FAITH VERSUS THE SECRETARIAT

You and I, having lived a little longer, are beginning to see a little further. For one thing, we have lived to see that vast Soviet collectivised empire, which so recently seemed poised to take over all the earth, stricken in its heartland, and forced to make agonising reappraisals of the militant ideology which was once the formula for universal conquest.

Yes! yes! it could be happening. In those last few years we may have witnessed the peak of Soviet-Marxist ideological penetration and the beginning of its decline. The Soviets themselves have no more dramatic ideas or world-beating philosophies to offer. *Only the*

Fabian-humanist elites entrenched within our Western democracies, and particularly within the Anglo-Saxon group of peoples, can assist them at this stage to snatch our defeat from the jaws of victory.

So where, and upon what issue, did the tide turn? Even after the brutal military clampdown of mid-December 1981, some commentators might agree that it started in Poland. A group of workers, defying the portended horrors of the salt mine, the labour camp or the psychiatric clinic, formed themselves into a free trade union, and achieved such an instantaneous response from millions of their compatriots that the Communist authorities were unable to contain it. Lech Walesa and his Solidarity Union became for a time the unlikely heroes of a counter-revolution which ultimately outreached itself, but which in a more disciplined form might go on spreading and developing, no matter how many tanks the military might range against it.

A band of horny-handed, materially impoverished working men had done what all the prestigious agencies of the West had failed to do in thirty years of "containing" Communism. They had done it in a situation where a single movement of the Bear's massive paw could have crushed them out of existence. But they had dared, — and against all the odds they had for a while succeeded, — because the spirit which sustained them was not buoyed up by material considerations alone.

Behind the men of Solidarity stood a revived Roman Catholic Church, which had somehow emerged from the draconian persecutions of Stalin's day with its faith unshaken and its roots strengthened within the hearts of the people. It is perhaps no mere coincidence that they made their stand less than two years after the Cardinal-Archbishop of Cracow had gone to Rome to become the first non-Italian pope since the Middle Ages.

Many Vatican-watchers, fearful that the Soviets might one day establish one of their own kind in the Holy See, must have wondered at the choice of Cardinal Wojtyla from Communist Poland. But as time went on the charismatic priest from Cracow looked more and more like a true man of God. It did not prevent him from becoming the target of an assassin's gun, and in May of 1981 he sustained wounds from which it took some time to recover. But here was a pastor who had somehow managed to live with the Communist domination of his native land without compromising his spiritual beliefs, and whilst protecting his flock from the vagaries and prejudices of a secular state bureaucracy. It is claimed that when he re-visited Poland as Pope John Paul II in 1979, twelve million people attended his services.

So it was in the wake of a heartwarming Christian revival that the men of Solidarity braved the secret police and the repression of the military. They did so, not as mere cogs in a totalitarian machine, but as individuals with immortal souls and individual hopes and aspirations. In their hearts they knew that there was a Higher Power than the local secretariat or the army HQ.

It was a development which would have shaken Big Brother if Orwell had anticipated its advent on the road to 1984. It is also the dread which pursues our humanist One Worlders, — that though they might wrap up the social, political and ecclesiastical establishments, and monitor them so closely as to bar all prospect of a reversal, they might yet be challenged by some unknown Messiah who would rise from the pit of defeat and degradation, and sweep their tawdry humanised philosophy into oblivion.

¶ 140 CLEANSING THE TEMPLE

And so, as we flay about us in frustration and disappointment, as our false gods and our idols come crashing about our ears, how best can we utilise our new-found awareness of the real problems confronting our generation? We are assuredly not all bible-thumping, hymn-singing Christians, but together we have stumbled on a vital truth, — that the Christian ethic, upon which our Western civilisation is founded, is simply not a transferable asset to be bought and sold in the exchanges, — that if we lose our divinely inspired faith, we lose also our standards and our values, and most likely our freedom.

Our senses dulled by the doctrine of conformity, many of us may have reckoned from time to time that it didn't make all that difference. But now we know the magnitude of our error, don't we? And if we are men and women of courage and conviction, we should know also that our eleventh-hour enlightenment is not a cosy little morsel of personal wisdom to be tucked away and only brought forth in congenial surroundings. It is meant to be aired and brandished abroad, thrust in the teeth of the humanist oligarchs, used like a scourge or a flailing broom till we have swept the Beast and his ecclesiastical charlatans right out of the Temple.

THE END

BIBLIOGRAPHY

"The SIECUS Circle" by Claire Chambers, Western Islands.

"Why Are You Losing Your Children?" by Barbara Morris.

"Where have all the children gone?" by Edward S. Williams, Ernest Stanton (Publishers), Johannesburg.

"The Fraudulent Gospel" by Bernard Smith, The Foreign Affairs Publishing Co., 139 Petersham Road, Richmond, Surrey.

"Keynes at Harvard" by Zygmund Dobbs, Probe Research Inc., West Sayville, New York 11796.

"The Terror Network" by Claire Sterling, Weidenfield (Publishers) Ltd.

"Nicaragua Betrayed" by ex-President Anastasio Somoza, Western Islands.

"All About Me" (Teacher's Guide to Early Schooling), published, Thomas Nelson & Sons Ltd., for the Schools Council.

"The Mind Benders" "The Lemming Folk" by James Gibb Stuart, William Maclellan (Embryo) Ltd.

"Christian Terror" by Father Arthur Lewis, Mardon Printers Ltd., Salisbury, Rhodesia.

INDEX OF PERSONS AND ORGANISATIONS